Working Like a Dog

THE STORY OF WORKING DOGS THROUGH HISTORY

GENA K. GORRELL

Tundra Books

For Fritz, Ophelia, Ulysses,

Geordie, Jasper, Rosie, Tara, and all the rest –

they also serve who only stand and wag.

Copyright © 2003 by Gena K. Gorrell

Published in Canada by Tundra Books,
481 University Avenue, Toronto, Ontario M5G 2E9

Published in the United States by Tundra Books of Northern New York,
P.O. Box 1030, Plattsburgh, New York 12901

Library of Congress Control Number: 2002117463

National Library of Canada Cataloguing in Publication

Gorrell, Gena K. (Gena Kinton), 1946-
  Working like a dog : the story of working dogs through history / Gena K. Gorrell.

Includes index.
ISBN 0-88776-589-0

  1. Working dogs – Juvenile literature. I. Title.

SF428.2.G67 2003   j636.73   C2003-900059-1

We acknowledge the financial support of the Government of Canada through the Book Publishing Industry Development Program (BPIDP) and that of the Government of Ontario through the Ontario Media Development Corporation's Ontario Book Initiative. We further acknowledge the support of the Canada Council for the Arts and the Ontario Arts Council for our publishing program.

Design: Blaine Herrmann
Printed and bound in Canada

1 2 3 4 5 6   08 07 06 05 04 03

CONTENTS

Outside of a dog, a book is man's best friend.
Inside of a dog, it's too dark to read.
— Groucho Marx

INTRODUCTION

Have you ever watched a dog walking beside his owners, and carrying his own leash in his mouth? Have you seen the *grin* on that dog's face? I think it's because the dog is working. *Boy, they're lucky I'm here to carry this leash.* . . . Dogs seem happiest when they're doing a job, and when they know they're doing it well.

Cats are another story. It's not that they won't work, but – you might say they're self-employed. Fluffy may run her paws off catching mice today, if she's in the mood, but tomorrow it's *Mouse? What mouse? I don't see any mouse. . . .*

For thousands of years, we humans have been taking advantage of the dog's determination to serve. We use dogs to help us in every way we can think of. Some of the jobs we give them are really cute. Some of the jobs are really hard. Some of the jobs kill them.

And here they are, after all this time – still with that big goofy grin, still ready to do anything we ask them to.

Why do they do it?

How – and when – did all this start?

CHAPTER ONE

In from the Cold

From high on a hillside, brother and sister watch the valley below. The Tall Ones are down there, doing strange things, as usual. The youngsters are fearful of the Tall Ones, but they are hollow with hunger, and their mouths water at the smell of food wafting up from the valley.

"I'm going down there," says the brother. "Come on."

"But what if they . . .?" His sister sniffs the air once more and relents. Together the two wolf cubs pad warily down the hill, toward the cooking-fire of the Stone Age family below.

How long have dogs been part of our lives? How many centuries ago did the first dog sneak off with the family's dinner (*Who, me?*) or snuggle into the family bedding (*Aw, please. It's cold out there*)? We really don't know.

The dog family is part of a larger animal family known as canids. The Latin name for the dog is *Canis familiaris*: "common canid" or – more appropriately – "household canid." Most experts on canine paleontology – the study of how the canid family developed – agree that dogs are descended from early wolves, and that wolves first appeared at least a million years ago. At some point – perhaps twenty or thirty thousand years ago – some wolves began to live with people, and the extraordinary partnership of humans and canids began.

Maybe it all started as we fought over fresh meat. Or maybe motherless cubs were adopted by a kind-hearted family. Or maybe, in times of hardship, we worked out some kind of cooperation that helped us both. We'll never be sure how wolves

The Canine Family Tree

To try to understand the huge variety of animals on our planet, we divide them into categories and sub-categories according to their anatomy and behavior. Dogs are a meat-eating, separate-toed sub-group of animals with backbones. Experts are still debating whether they are really a separate species, or just part of the wolf species.

Phylum   Chordata
(having a backbone or something similar)
|
Order   Carnivora
(mostly meat-eating)
|
Suborder   Fissipedia
(having separate toes)
|
Superfamily   Canidae
(dog type, not cat type)
|
Family   Dog
(also includes wolf, jackal, coyote)
|
Species   Canis Familiaris
(domestic dog)

and humans overcame their mutual suspicion, but we can guess this much: we came together partly because of the similarities between us.

Like people, wolves are social animals: they live in groups, with leaders and followers, and they help each other find food and raise families. Like our early ancestors, they often hunt animals much larger than themselves, using teamwork and persistence. Like us, they are constantly communicating with each other, by voice

🐾 *Why is it that we trust dogs with our lives, yet we accuse their close relative — the intelligent, sociable wolf — of everything from blowing down the little pig's straw house to menacing Red Riding Hood's grandmother?*

and body language. A wolf that made its way into a human community would soon understand the status of the various family members — who was senior, who was junior — and would learn the meanings of many human sounds, signals, and postures.

While our similarities may have helped bring us together, our diffe- rences have made our partnership even more valuable. We humans have sharp eyesight and excellent color vision, and the way our eyes are positioned on our head gives us a good sense of distance; wolves have keen night vision, and phenomenal powers of hearing and smell. We have the brains for imaginative long-range planning; the wolf has the muscles for speed and power. We have agile hands that are free to make and brandish weapons; the wolf grows fearsome weapons on jaws and feet. Together, what a team we make!

From Wolf to Dog

How did those early wolves turn into the immense range of dogs we have today, from miniature poodle to Great Dane? The process probably started when people were first settling into permanent communities. It's likely that some wolves learned to hang around these settlements, stealing meat and scavenging scraps of garbage.

🐾 *This primitive rock art from Tassili-n-ajer, in Algeria, shows people and canids hunting as a team in the Stone Age. The upcurved tails of the canids suggest that they are dogs, not wolves.*

As one litter after another was born on the edge of human society, probably only a few wolves were fearless enough to be comfortable so close to people, while the others retreated to the wild.

Did humans capture some of the wolf cubs and make them part of the family? Did a few wolves become so confident around people that they moved into the settlement of their own free will? However it happened, a number of these wolves who didn't mind people eventually started living inside the community and raising cubs there. Year after year, as generations of cubs grew up, the young wolves who were shy of people left the settlement and moved to the wild. The ones who were aggressive toward people were killed or driven away. Only a handful of the animals – those who were not too timid and not too aggressive – remained.

As these few wolves interbred among themselves, and passed their genes on to cubs and grandcubs, the generations came to look less and less like their cousins in the wild. Before long – perhaps within one human lifetime – these animals had an appearance and behavior that we today would recognize as doglike.

Why did they change so much? Many explanations have been suggested for how each separate change – in size, color, teeth, and so on – may have helped them fit better into human society. But the answer may be even simpler. When genetic information (DNA) is passed from parents to children, certain characteristics that appear to be unrelated are in fact linked together – that is, a child who inherits one characteristic is likely to inherit the linked ones as well. (For example, some breeds of dog have a genetic link between deafness and white hair; the white puppies in a litter are more likely to be deaf.) It's possible that when the temperament of the village wolves was evolving to be more domesticated, a number of other characteristics (size, color, teeth, etc.) were evolving too, because they happened to be genetically linked to temperament.

The Wolf That Wasn't

Meanwhile, in the isolated continent of Australia, marsupials were evolving. Marsupials are a kind of mammal, but unlike most mammals, they are born very tiny and they develop further in the mother's pouch. (Kangaroos and koalas are marsupials.) In time, Australia's marsupials had much the same variety as the mammals elsewhere – there were big ones, small ones, grazing ones, preying ones – so it's not surprising that one of them, the thylacine, looked and acted very much like a wolf.

Thylacines seem to have been successful hunters until a few thousand years ago, when disaster struck: some primitive dogs arrived in Australia, probably brought by seafarers trading with the Aboriginals who lived there. The dogs multiplied and many became feral (wild), competing for the same prey as the thylacines. The dogs won the contest, and their descendants in Australia today are the wolflike canids known as dingoes.

Some dingoes live with Aboriginal families, but many remain feral; they nest in burrows or hollow tree trunks, and tend to howl rather than bark. Like wolves, they have only one litter of pups a year, while most breeds of dog can have two. Even the dingoes who live around people stay fairly independent, and it's almost impossible to train them. Did the dingo never quite become domesticated? Or did it evolve into a dog and then, in Australia's barren outback, start turning wolflike again?

As for the thylacine, it became extinct in Australia. A small population survived for a while in Tasmania, an island south of Australia that remained dog-free for many years. Indeed, there are still rumors of a few wild thylacines lurking in the Tasmanian wilderness. But the last known thylacine died in a zoo in 1936.

Settling the Great Dog Fight

There is still a lot of argument about the origins of today's dogs. Since different kinds of wolves lived in different parts of the world, some people think that a

❧ The dingo (left) remains more wolflike than most dogs, in both appearance and behavior. As for the thylacine, even if we never find any surviving in the wild, there is a small chance that the one who died in 1936 (right) will not be the last of her kind. Several thylacine fetuses were preserved in laboratory jars of alcohol, and alcohol does not destroy DNA. Will we someday clone new thylacines from the genes of these long-dead infants?

number of human communities developed partnerships with whatever wolves happened to be nearby, and that those various wolves evolved into dogs of one sort or another. Others believe that certain breeds developed not from wolves but from jackals (who are smaller than wolves and live in hotter countries) or other canids. Yet others are convinced that the dog species evolved without human influence, and that it was early dogs – not their wolf or jackal ancestors – who gave up their freedom to sit by our cooking-fires.

In those days the continents of our planet were connected more than they are now, so it was easier for people to trek from one land mass to another – from Asia to the Americas, for example. When they went, they took their animals with them.

When they traded pots and tools with neighboring tribes, they must sometimes have used pups for trading as well. All this travel and trading made it hard for researchers to trace the change from wolf (or wolves) to different kinds of dog. Until recently, they could only look at the bones and teeth and hair of ancient canids, and compare them to those of modern dogs and wolves.

Now studies using the latest DNA technology are comparing the genetic material of various dogs and wolves and early canine remains. These studies seem to suggest that all the dogs in the world developed from just one species, a kind of wolf who lived in East Asia. Further research should give us a "map" of all the chromosomes in dogs, to help scientists pinpoint the genes responsible for a dog's looks and behavior, and for certain diseases. We may also be able to settle, for once and for all, the argument about where and when our two species came together.

For now, though, we have good evidence that dogs – no longer wolves – were living in human camps at least fifteen thousand years ago. They probably acted as sentries, warning the families if an intruder appeared. They cleaned up food garbage lying around camp, which might have attracted dangerous animals, and they were playmates for small children. When we began raising domestic animals, dogs may have tended the flocks and herds. When we learned to make possessions like pottery and jewelry, the dogs may have scared away thieves.

Cities and Kingdoms

Century by century, our societies became more complex. We learned to build permanent homes, and to grow crops. We clustered our homes into towns, and towns grew into cities, and cities grew into states ruled by powerful leaders. More and more crafts developed: people learned to be shoemakers and sculptors, brewers and bakers, scribes and doctors, stonemasons and goldsmiths. The more complex life became, the more help we needed from our dogs – and the more kinds of dogs we needed.

The Days of the Pharaohs

By the time of ancient Egypt, about five thousand years ago, dogs were precious members of many families, especially rich ones. Wall paintings show household

🐾 *The Egyptian pharaoh Tutankhamen — the famous King Tut — was buried with a treasury of wonderful things, and in the entrance of his tomb was this handsome statue of the jackal god Anubis, draped in linen and perched on a gilded shrine containing jewelry. The hieroglyphic sign of a jackal on a shrine means "he who is over the secrets" — maybe a reference to the valuables within.*

dogs wearing elegant collars, and when pet dogs died they were sometimes buried with great ceremony, even preserved as mummies, while their owners shaved their heads to show their grief.

Egyptian dogs seem to have come in a number of shapes and sizes. There were tall, thin hunting hounds who lived in kennels and were trained and managed by hired dog-handlers. Large, muscular, square-headed dogs – rather like today's mastiff – were bred and trained for warfare, and released on the battlefield to savage the enemy with teeth and claws. As shrewd merchants added dogs to the list of foreign goods they imported, Egypt also gained a variety of small, short-legged dogs that snoozed under – or on – the furniture.

Because of their obedience and loyalty, and their devoted service, dogs were held up as an example of what every good servant owed his master – and what every good Egyptian owed the pharaoh, who was not only a king but a god as well. After all, the classic dog name, Fido, is Latin for "faithful."

But dogs were more than just servants; they had their link to godship too. The Egyptians had an extremely complex view of death and the afterlife, involving elaborate rituals. One of the main characters in this part of their mythology was the god Anubis, a black dog or jackal who was said to supervise the process of turning corpses into mummies, and to guard the land of the dead. When you died, it was Anubis who led your soul away and weighed your heart in a scale, against the feather of truth. If your heart weighed the same as the feather, you entered the eternal afterlife. If not, another god – part lion, part crocodile – gobbled up the heart.

Understandably people wanted to be on good terms with Anubis. Some of them crossbred their dogs with jackals, producing a jackal-dog in honor of Anubis. People would use a small dog-amulet of clay or metal as an offering to the god. They might even make a pilgrimage to the City of Dogs, to buy dog souvenirs, pay tribute at the dog-temples, and leave offerings to feed the priests and the city's huge canine population. Sometimes they bought a mummified dog and left it at the temple as an offering. (Unfortunately, this created a large demand for dog mummies. It seems that some temples ran a grisly business on the side, raising puppies and slaughtering them just to make mummies.)

Assyria

In the later days of ancient Egypt, the Assyrian Empire rose in the Middle East. The Assyrians were a warlike people. When the king was not away on a military campaign, he often went out with his nobles and servants and horses and dogs, to hunt lions and other wild animals. The royal hunt was not just an amusement. It was also a way to remind people that the king would be fierce and powerful in defending them if they were loyal – and in punishing them if they were not.

🐾 *The Assyrians are famous for their beautiful wall sculptures, like this portrayal of a muscular mastiff-type dog in the midst of King Ashurbanipal's royal hunt. The carving was done about 2,500 years ago, in the Assyrian capital city of Nineveh.*

Greece

After the days of the Assyrian Empire came the time of ancient Greece. The conqueror Alexander the Great spread Greek ideas and beliefs across Europe and Asia, and even as far as India. Like the early Egyptians, the Greeks believed in a host of gods and goddesses. Once again, dogs both profited and suffered from religion. During the festival of Artemis, the Greek goddess of the hunt, cattle, goats, and sheep were sacrificed, and wealthy hunters and their dogs feasted together on roast meat. But less valuable dogs were sacrificed by the thousands, to win some favor or other from the fickle gods.

Dogs played other roles in Greece, as well. On rocky hillsides, big, shaggy dogs stood guard over herds and flocks, wearing spiked leather collars to protect them from wolf attacks. If a wild animal was threatening flocks, strong nets were set up in a line, and dogs were sent to track the beast down and chase it into the nets, where it could be speared to death. Some towns kept dozens of night watchdogs to patrol the walls while the citizens slept. Tracking dogs pursued criminals and other fugitives. And many dogs lived in Greek homes as members of the family; they appear often in Greek art, not just as symbols of power or obedience but as realistic individuals with personality and emotion – in short, as friends.

Rome

Just before the dawn of the Christian era, the legions of the Roman army marched across Greece and the rest of Europe, invading the Middle East and North Africa, even crossing the English Channel to conquer the British Isles. The Romans were practical, acquisitive people, with an eye for international trade and technology. As their empire flourished, wealthy merchants and landowners competed for the grandest estates, the most lavish dinners, the most exquisite ornaments – and, of course, the most fashionable dogs. All across the empire, unusual dogs were interbred to create exotic new pets.

But Rome had working dogs too. As elsewhere, they served as bodyguards and watchdogs. They patrolled the long, straight roads that the Romans built across their spreading empire, and escorted the caravans traveling those roads. In conquered territories they guarded storehouses and weapons arsenals against rebellious locals. There were herding dogs, and draft dogs to carry or pull loads, and, as always, there were hunting dogs – not only hounds, but pointers to show where the prey was, and retrievers to bring it back. There were also fearless little dogs who chased small prey to earth wherever it tried to hide – perhaps the ancestors of the terriers we have today.

One dog especially valued was the Molossus, who could weigh more than 250 pounds (110 kg), and was strong enough and fast enough to knock an enemy off his horse and rip him to pieces. Whole battalions of these dogs were trained by the army, and sent into battle wearing collars with long, sharp spikes to slash the legs of enemy horses, and sometimes padded armor as well. (Early war dogs were often turned into killing machines. Some had lances mounted on their backs, to spear any horses and soldiers who got in their way. Others had firepots of smoke and flame strapped to their backs, to panic the enemy's horses and scorch their bellies.) A Roman military writer named Blondus said that such a dog should be so ferocious that "he will not allow himself to be stroked even by those he knows best, but threatens everybody alike with the fulminations of his teeth, and always looks at everybody as though he is burning with anger." Molossus dogs were even released in arenas to fight wild animals (or each other) to the death, or to slaughter helpless prisoners in the bloody executions that served as public entertainment.

The Dogs of Death

Egypt was by no means the only place where a dog controlled the path to the after-life. According to the ancient Greeks, Cerberus, a monstrous many-headed dog, guarded the far shore of the River Styx, boundary of the underworld. Some natives of North America said that dogs guarded the bridge over the river of death, deciding whether or not the deceased deserved eternal life. In South America, the Aztecs told of a dog-headed god named Xolotl who helped the dead across a similar river. The Chukchi people of Siberia believed that the demon of death hunted people down with a hound. Welsh stories said that when someone was dying, the hounds of hell would scratch and whine at the door until the soul came away with them. The myths of Iceland said that the barking of a dog named Garm would herald the end of the entire world.

🐾 *Hades, the king of the underworld, with a three-headed Cerberus. (In some stories Cerberus has fifty heads.) This carving – in the ancient Parthian city of Hatra, in Iraq – was done about two thousand years ago. Rome had conquered Greece by then, but the gods worshipped in many places were still essentially Greek, despite their local costumes.*

Why did so many cultures believe that when a soul set off on its last journey, a dog would be involved somewhere along the way? Maybe it was because dogs faithfully accompany us in life, or because they often guard doorways, or maybe it had to do with dogs' uncanny ability to find their way home.

But dogs were associated with death for other, darker reasons. In the days before medical science, disease was a mysterious curse, and deadly epidemics seemed to spring up out of nowhere. Naturally, people looked for someone to blame. The pets and hunting dogs of the upper classes might be above suspicion, but there were plenty of homeless dogs – pariah dogs – in the streets. (Pariahs are outcasts shunned by society.) These dogs lived on the rotting garbage discarded by people, as their ancestors had done for thousands of years. But they also ate dead or dying animals. Many people claimed that when the dreaded plague swept through town and unburied corpses piled up in the streets, the pariah dogs ate those too. If dogs could be so gruesomely involved in the tragedy, it was all too easy to believe that, somehow, they had caused it.

To make matters worse, people knew even then that dogs – like many other animals – could carry rabies. One bite from a nervous pet was enough to spread the disease, and rabies victims died a slow and horrible death. Numerous cures were suggested through the ages, using such medications as dog hairs, puppy livers, salt and vinegar, or olive oil and garlic. One French writer suggested in the 1300s that the victim find a rooster, "pluck its backside . . . and to the bite wound or wounds apply the anus of the bird which will suck out the poison."

Rabies vaccination would not be invented until the late 1800s. Until then, when one dog became rabid, thousands of others might be killed to prevent the spread of the disease. Sometimes the dogs were massacred on a mistaken suspicion that one of them had rabies. Sometimes the extermination was carried out because someone in power just didn't like dogs.

Godless Dogs

While many church leaders adored their own pet dogs, the official religious view of dogs was confusing and even contradictory. In the Jewish tradition dogs were thought to be unclean – perhaps because the corpses sometimes thrown to them were considered unclean – but they were tolerated because it wasn't their fault; they were as God had made them.

Similarly, the Islamic religion recognized dogs as Allah's creatures, yet saw them as so tainted that any strict Muslim who touched one needed a ritual cleansing. But since high-ranking Muslims enjoyed the hunt as much as their Christian peers, their favorite hunting dogs, Salukis, were reclassified as – well, not *really* dogs.

The official Christian view was equally muddled. On one hand, dogs were sometimes abhorred as brutish and unclean, and it was seen as sinful to "waste" love on a dog instead of saving it for God and family. Some dogs were accused of being demons in disguise, serving as witches' "familiars" (assistants). On the other hand, a number of saints – including Hubert, the patron saint of hunters – are usually portrayed with a dog. The symbol of Saint Bernard of Clairvaux is a white dog. Saint Dominic de Guzman, founder of the Dominican religious order, is shown with a dog and a globe; indeed, Dominican friars are sometimes called *Domini canem*: "dogs of God," faithful to their Master's will.

Celebrated as deities, slaughtered as pestilent vermin, condemned as devil-spawn, cherished as man's best friend – when those first wolves ventured into the circle of human company so many thousands of years ago, who could have imagined what they were getting themselves into?

CHAPTER TWO

Tools and Toys

Anoint [a sick Pekingese dog] with the clarified fat of the leg of a
snow-leopard and give it to drink from song thrush egg-shells full of
juice of custard apples, in which are three pinches of shredded
rhinoceros horn. . . .   *— Tz'u-hsi, Dowager Empress of China*

Silk was ancient China's treasure, and its secret. Some two thousand years ago, caravans were crossing Asia to reach the Middle East and Europe, where the lustrous fabric sold for immense prices. But only the silk was for sale. The Chinese penalty for exporting silkworm eggs – which would allow Westerners to breed silkworms and make their own silk – was death.

When the trade wagons went back to China, they carried goods in return. Among the exotic novelties were small dogs from Europe and some lions from India. The dogs created a sensation at the royal court. The lions were more significant, though, because they were symbols of Buddhism, which was spreading through China at the time. It was said that Buddha flew through the air on a lion's back; when he descended to earth, the lion shrank to be tiny enough to ride inside his sleeve. It was also said that Buddha could conjure up thousands of tiny lions that whirled together into one great lion, to attack his enemies.

Then someone came up with a daring idea: why not mold these cute little dogs into tiny lions?

Anxious to please the emperor, imperial dog-breeders began changing the dogs' color and form by selective breeding – that is, they chose the male and female dogs

❀ *In Europe, the little lion-dogs were called Pekinese or Pekingese, after China's capital city of Peking (now Beijing). At first the puppies were purposely deformed into the desired shape, but eventually selective breeding created a size and shape that was inherited from generation to generation. Some dogs (such as Chihuahuas) have been bred for miniaturization, which reduces the dog's size but keeps the parts in proportion; others (like the bulldog) have been bred for dwarfism, which makes the legs so short that they are no longer in proportion to the head and torso. Pekingese have been both miniaturized and dwarfed.*

who were closest to what they wanted and bred them, and from the resulting litters they picked out puppies who were even closer to what they wanted and bred them, and so on, generation after generation.

Since selective breeding takes years, though, the breeders also looked for faster solutions. They starved the puppies to keep them small, and dressed them in wire corsets to deform their bones. One way and another, they produced "sleeve dogs" tiny enough to ride in a court lady's costume and keep her hands warm, and dogs in "lucky" colors. Turning the canine face into a catlike one was more difficult, but by mashing the puppy's nose in and stretching the tongue out, they managed to create a dog who looked – a little – like a miniature lion.

About 1,500 years ago, China lost its precious monopoly. Silkworm eggs were smuggled out of China, and other nations were finally able to produce their own silk. Now the little lion-dogs were the secret Chinese treasure. They were closely guarded, and there were fierce penalties for selling them without royal permission. At the imperial court, the pampered animals were bathed and perfumed by countless servants, and carried from place to place on cushions of silk, or in elaborate cages bright with enamelwork and jade.

There were larger dogs at the Chinese court as well. The emperors went tiger-hunting with dogs much like today's greyhounds and mastiffs. One very early ruler was buried with his hunting dog, who wore a collar of gold, silver, and turquoise. A sixth-century emperor appointed his favorite dogs to noble rank, equal to duke or viceroy, and the thirteenth-century traveler Marco Polo reported that the Chinese emperor of his day employed a staff of twenty thousand – half dressed in scarlet, the other half in blue – to care for his great hunting dogs.

There were also humbler dogs at work. Chows traditionally served as town watchdogs, and guarded junks (houseboats). Dogs pulled sledges, or went to war. As elsewhere, they were sacrificed to win favors from the gods; for example, spilling the blood of a white dog at the gates of a city was supposed to keep the citizens safe. And certain dogs were raised for meat – not just in times of starvation, but as a special delicacy.

Bones of Contention

Dog meat has been a delicacy in a number of cultures, including early Greece and Rome. Dogs are still eaten in some countries, to the disgust of many Westerners. But then, devout Hindus are repelled by the idea of eating beef, observant Jews and Muslims recoil from a plate of pork, and other people limit themselves to poultry, or to fish, or to egg and dairy products, or abhor any food that comes from animals. Perhaps, for the time being, we should keep our noses out of each other's plates, and worry more about how we treat animals while they are alive.

🐾 *Archduke Albrecht — son of Maximilian II, ruler of the Holy Roman Empire in the 1500s. The scallop badge on his dog's collar is a reassuring Catholic emblem; Maximilian had almost lost his chance at the throne because he was suspected of being Protestant. Perhaps his subjects were reassured to know that even the family dog was Catholic!*

Chiens de Luxe

In Europe, as in China, some lucky dogs lived regally. Louis XI of France adored his greyhound Cherami (the name means "dear friend") and dressed him in a collar of red velvet covered in pearls and rubies. In England around the same time, the dogs of Henry VIII sported embroidered collars hung with pearls and pendants. Some royal pets paraded in robes of velvet or embroidered satin; some wore perfume, and earrings, and diamond lockets.

It's not surprising that high-ranking people often doted on their dogs. At a time when many children died young, the heirs to titles and large estates had to be isolated from other children so they wouldn't catch dangerous infections. A fashionable dog, properly groomed and tended by the servants, was a much-needed playmate. Some princes learned to ride when they were still toddlers, straddling their dogs in place of ponies. One little French prince learned to hunt in the palace ballroom, setting his pet dogs on small prey; he was a skilled hunter by the time he became King Louis XIII at the age of nine.

Since the upper classes enjoyed hunting, they liked to reserve the pleasure – and the game animals – for themselves. There were often laws against peasants hunting, or even owning a dog who might bring home dinner. In twelfth-century England, common dogs living near forests were measured by foot size; if the front feet were large, the middle toes were chopped off so the dog couldn't run well enough to catch anything. In sixteenth-century France, a bishop had a poacher (illegal hunter) tied up in a deerskin and tossed to the hounds. Yet poaching remained common practice; even the king's own swans could end up on a humble dinner table.

When they were old enough, children of exalted families were matched in strategic marriages, sometimes to people they hadn't even met. The husbands then busied themselves with matters of estate and kingdom – or with other ladies of the court – while the wives endured one pregnancy after another. Since many babies died, and those who didn't were whisked off to be reared by servants, a noble lady might have little consolation except her darling doggies.

Sometimes the dogs gave physical relief, as well as companionship. Whether she was a queen or a mere attendant, a lady of the court had duties to perform. Aches, cramps, and minor pains were no excuse for her absence. The warmth of a small dog could be very soothing – and surely a soft, snuggling pet was more endearing than the rubber hot-water bottle used by later generations.

Even kings found rare comfort in their dogs. Surrounded by schemers and spies, where else could they turn for honest, unselfish devotion? Besides, dogs were useful, and not just for hunting. In the bedchamber, a large dog made a trustworthy body-guard. At dinner, a small dog could taste each dish before it was served, in case it was poisoned; sometimes the dog perched right on the table. (In a time when fingers were used more than forks, a table dog also came in handy as a napkin.) And how could any court be fashionable unless it had all the latest dogs?

As always, though, there was a dark side. Downstairs, in the sweltering kitchens, dogs and servants labored together to prepare lavish dinners. Enormous haunches

🐾 *Dog power was used to pump water, to grind grain, and to press juice out of apples for cider. Dogs would go on working as kitchen servants for centuries. This 1850s advertisement is selling a dog-powered churn; by walking on the treadmill, the dog whips cream into butter.*

of meat were roasted in the hearth, on a spit over a wood fire, and in many grand homes the spit was rotated by a small dog – called a turnspit – trudging in weary circles on a treadwheel like the exercise wheel in a hamster's cage. Terriers and other small dogs paced the dark corners of homes and warehouses, killing mice, rats, and other vermin.

Dying for Fun

Some dogs faced more fearsome opponents. If it was good sport to watch a pack of hunting dogs chase a deer through the forest and tear it to pieces, it was more convenient – especially in nasty weather – to bring the spectacle indoors. Gaming pits (arenas) were built, and packs of tough, aggressive dogs were raised as killers, trained to attack stags, bulls, wild boar, or even horses, while the cream of society watched and placed bets and cheered on their favorites.

🐾 *In an age when entertainment was hard to come by, many poor people imitated the gaming of the wealthy. They trained dogs to fight rats, or each other, and gambled on the outcome. One terrier, Manchester Billy, was famous for killing a hundred rats in less than seven minutes — about one rat every four seconds. This picture shows an English dogfight around 1800. The brutality of dogfighting still goes on, although it is illegal in many countries.*

The gaming pits gave pit-bull dogs their name, and the compact, sturdy breed we know as bulldogs were indeed developed to tackle bulls:

> Enraged bulls charged with their heads down. In order to avoid the lethal horns, the dogs had to be low to the ground and relatively nimble. Because a bull was most vulnerable on its tender nose, the bulldog needed strong jaws as well as the dumb courage to jump at the bull's face and the perseverance to hang on.

Even the bulldog's squashed-in face reflects this bull-baiting past; the dogs were bred to have widely spaced nostrils, placed far back on the snout, so they could breathe without letting go of the bull.

Dogs were wounded, dogs were killed, but eventually the target animal would be ripped apart. At one of these "baitings" staged for England's Queen Elizabeth I, sixteen red deer were slaughtered by the royal greyhounds; at another, dogs mauled thirteen bears to death in the name of sport. For a celebration in 1623, a white bear was driven into the Thames River, "where the dogs baited him swimming; which was the best sport of all." By the 1700s, even lions and tigers were being imported for the sport.

Dogs across the Atlantic

Dogs were living with the people of the Americas long before Europeans arrived. It's not clear whether they evolved from American wolves or came from other continents thousands of years earlier, along with migrating tribes, but they played many of the same roles as in Europe; they were playmates, watchdogs, and hunting companions. They could track deer, moose, bear, or caribou, and hold them at bay until the hunters arrived with their spears. Since the natives had no horses before the Europeans came, dogs often served as draft animals, carrying loads, or hauling them on a toboggan or travois.

Life could be hard in the wilderness, though, and people couldn't afford to waste anything. Among some tribes, dogs – especially white ones – were sacrificed before the hunt, to ensure a good catch. Clothing or even windows could be made from dogskins, and mattresses could be stuffed with dog hair. In some places people raised "wool dogs" with soft, thick hair, shearing them like sheep each time the hair was long enough, and weaving it into coats and blankets. Dogs were helpful in all kinds of ways.

But as the countries of Europe squabbled over the wealth and territory of the Americas – as explorers and adventurers crossed the ocean to find their fortunes, and brought their dogs with them – some of these European dogs were turned into vicious weapons against the native people.

In 1494, when Christopher Columbus landed in Jamaica and encountered a party of natives, he set a large dog on them; several of the natives were killed. The next year, in Haiti, local people tried to remove a religious cross the Europeans had erected, and a pack of twenty dogs tore them apart. When the Spanish began mining

🐾 This 1885 sketch shows a Cree couple on the move, with the family dog dragging some of their belongings on a travois — two long poles fastened to the dog, with one or more loads secured across the poles. Sometimes the load was slung in a large net or woven basket. A dog could pull about fifty pounds (23 kg) of baggage.

precious metals in South America in the 1500s, they used *perros de sangre* (dogs of blood) to control their slave laborers and keep them from escaping. Sometimes they set dogs to attack the natives just for sport – as they had done with bears and wild boars at home – ignoring the dismayed protests of their own priests.

Dog Meets Dog

As European families began moving to North America, their dogs came along too, to help in the hunt and herd domestic animals. The dogs protected the settlers against wolves and bears, and warned them of attacks by rival Europeans, or by native people. Most of all, they were trusted friends in this strange and untamed land.

Ever since Europeans had first arrived in North America, native people had been trading animal pelts – bear, fox, beaver, lynx, and whatever else they could hunt or trap – for imported tools, hunting weapons, fabrics, and small luxuries. Since many of the European dogs looked strange and exotic to the natives, they became trade goods too. A dog whose ancestors had guarded a British fortress or a French château might now snooze outside a tipi, dreaming of buffalo bones. As dogs of the Old World interbred with those of the New World – and sometimes with wolves and coyotes – their sizes, shapes, and personalities became even more varied.

Dogs did their share of exploring, too. At the start of the 1800s, the American government didn't know much about the country west of the Mississippi River. There were tales of crystal mountains and golden cliffs, of unicorns, of beavers larger than people. An army captain, Meriwether Lewis, was asked to lead a party across this mysterious land, to discover the truth and get acquainted with the native people. Lewis chose some thirty companions, including his friend William Clark. Lewis also took along his dog, Scammon, described in his diary as "of the new-foundland breed very active strong and docile." The burly, deep-voiced dog proved his value to the Lewis and Clark expedition through almost eight thousand miles (13,000 km) of prairie, river, and mountains. He scared off persistent grizzly bears and a buffalo that charged through the camp. When the men shot geese for dinner, he leapt into the water to retrieve them. When squirrels were seen swimming across a river, "I made my dog take as many each day as I had occasion for," Lewis noted;

Scammon caught the squirrels in the water and brought them back to the boat, where they were fried for dinner. It's no wonder that when a native offered to buy Scammon for three beaverskins, Lewis wouldn't give up his valuable dog.

The Lifeguard Dogs

Where did the huge Newfoundland dogs – like Lewis's – originate? Their ancestors may have come from Europe five hundred years ago, with the sailing fleets that fished the Grand Banks off the eastern coast of North America. The Vikings may have brought dogs to the area another five hundred years before that. And dogs may have lived with the native people even earlier.

Whoever their ancestors were, today's Newfoundlands are impressively well equipped for maritime work, even on the cold, stormy North Atlantic. With their massive size and strong hind legs, they are tireless swimmers. Their webbed toes give them added power in the water, and help them walk over soft, squishy mudbanks. Their warm, thick inner coat is protected by an oily outer coat that keeps them dry.

🐾 *A Newfoundland "on duty" on a ship's prow. When Portuguese fleets began fishing off the coast of North America, large water dogs were part of the team. They swam out to the nets, caught the cork floats in their jaws, and dragged the nets back through the surf to shore. The dogs also retrieved things that fell off the boats, and even carried messages from boat to boat.*

Since these dauntless animals spend so much time on ships and around shore, and have such a passion for leaping into the water and retrieving just about anything, it's not surprising that there are hundreds of tales of them saving people from drowning. Someone slips and falls into the sea – a jet-black blur streaks into the water, swims out to seize a sleeve or collar – and the victim is towed to safety. (These self-appointed lifeguards have also "rescued" some very startled swimmers!)

Many of these powerful dogs also worked on land. In summer they hauled cartloads of fish from the docks for processing, or dragged logs from the forest to the sawmill. They did such a fine job of delivering mail to the outports (isolated villages) of Newfoundland that they were portrayed on several postage stamps.

Times Change

As European settlements spread farther and farther across North America, and forests were turned into farms and cities, dogs did many of the same draft jobs they did in Europe. In the countryside, a traveling workman like a knife-sharpener or tinker (pot-mender) might have a dog to carry his tools and metal supplies. In the city, in a time before refrigerators and freezers, dog carts made daily deliveries of fresh milk and meat. The carts could pass through laneways too narrow for a horse and wagon. While the merchant was dealing with customers, the dog would guard the loaded cart. Often, though, these dogs were terribly abused. Overworked and underfed, they were forced through long hours of hard labor, and kicked or clubbed or even stabbed when they were too tired to go on.

During the 1800s, there was a growing social and political movement against cruelty and injustice. Many people became deeply troubled about the way some humans, and some animals, were being mistreated. At the same time, more people were becoming middle class, with enough money to include a pet dog or two in the family. There were angry arguments, and newspaper articles and public speeches, about the miserable life draft dogs so often lived, and many places passed laws controlling the use of draft dogs, or banning them altogether.

While dogs were winning protection against vicious people, some people were finally being saved from vicious dogs. Beginning in the 1500s, thousands of shiploads of Africans had been captured and shipped over as slaves so the American

🐾 *A dog in Quebec pulls a load of dried codfish. Notice that the dog's head is slightly out of focus. Until fast films were developed, it was hard to keep a dog still long enough to take a good picture. That's why Fido often appears in painted family portraits but is almost always missing from early photographic portraits.*

colonies would have cheap labor, especially on the great plantations of the southern states. These states continued to use slaves after the practice was abolished in the north. When slaves tried to escape to the north, where they might find freedom, their irate "masters" could hire slave-catchers and slave-hunting dogs to hunt down the fugitives and drag them back. And if the runaways were sometimes killed by the dogs, that was a sharp warning to any other slave who dreamed of freedom. In 1865 slavery was finally outlawed in the southern states as well, putting the slave-catchers and their dogs out of work.

By this time, there were also great changes taking place on the far side of the globe. The imperial grandeur of China was beginning to crumble, and Western nations were forcing the Chinese to end their isolation and open their country to foreign trade. Armies and gunboats attacked Chinese cities, and in 1860 the English and French plundered the glorious Summer Palace, near Beijing, and burned it to the ground. Among the prizes looted from the palace was a small Pekingese. An English captain named the dog Looty and presented it to Queen Victoria, an ardent dog-fancier.

More and more Pekingese made their way to the West, stolen or smuggled out of China. A few were even given to Westerners by Tz'u-hsi, the Dowager Empress of China, although she made sure the dogs were neutered first so they couldn't be bred. With their elegant looks and royal connections, the dogs became wildly fashionable in Europe.

Just as well; in 1912 the Chinese empire was overthrown and China became a republic. In their homeland the once precious pets were now despised as symbols of the old aristocracy, and many were slaughtered. In Europe, however, the Pekingese lived on – still petted and pampered; still meticulously bred for tiny size, and fashionable shape and color; still fancifully imagined as little lions.

The Pekinese
Abstain from fleas
    And doggy things like that,
But hate it when
Unthinking men
    Compare them to the cat.

CHAPTER THREE

Doing What Comes Naturally

Every true man and every true woman loves a noble dog, and there are no more splendid dogs in all the world than those magnificent brutes of Whale Sound. Perhaps my reader may think me prejudiced. I have a right to be. They saved my life and the lives of my two comrades.

– Robert E. Peary, Arctic explorer

By the early 1900s, dogs were being replaced in many jobs by new technology. More and more people gave up farming to work in factories, where dog-power wasn't needed. Pumps and presses were converted to steam power and, later, to electrical power. Cows and sheep were sent to market by truck or train. Lumberjacks hitched their logs to tractors. Tradesmen loaded their tools and wares into new-fangled automobiles.

Still, many dogs went on doing pretty much the same jobs they had done for thousands of years. They guarded people, places, and property. They shared the hunt. In the course of protecting livestock and chasing down prey, some breeds developed amazing skill in herding. And dogs continued to haul loads in regions where automobiles and larger draft animals weren't practical.

Cave Canem

This warning – Latin for "Beware of the dog" – has been posted outside homes since

Herr Dobermann's Doberman

In the late 1800s, a German tax collector named Louis Dobermann needed protection on his rounds. He mixed a number of breeds and came up with a dog who was big enough and tough enough to defend him from reluctant taxpayers. Today's lean, muscular Doberman pinscher, developed from Herr Dobermann's dog, is one of many breeds keeping watch in banks and showrooms, and sniffing out intruders in factories, warehouses, and scrapyards. Some-times the dogs accompany the night guard; often they *are* the night guard. They see better than we do in dim light, and their ears are more sensitive to slight differences in sound. Snoozing with one eye open, they keep their ears pricked for the scratch of metal on metal or the crack of breaking glass. Why would anyone break into premises defended by the sharp ears and nose – not to mention teeth – of a well-trained guard dog?

Roman times. (It's been suggested that for some lazy pets, "Beware you don't *trip over* the dog" would be more apt.) Just as wolves watch for intruders and alert the pack to a suspicious presence, so dogs tend to react to the sound or smell of a stranger. Today, as in the past, most dogs defend their own family and domain, whether it's the geese in the farmyard, the sheep in the pasture, or the plaster gnomes on the lawn. Some work in the family business, guarding the shop all day and escorting the day's proceeds to the bank at night. Others are employed as sentries and bodyguards for businesses and security companies.

Ron Minion used to be a police-dog handler for the Royal Canadian Mounted Police. Now he runs a private security company with a dozen dogs. He breeds most of his dogs himself, and personally trains his security guards in dog-handling. The dogs are taught to be multi-handler – that is, they live at company headquarters under the care of a dogmaster, and they can work with any of the handlers. "But sometimes," he says, "a dog and handler just fall in love, and the dog ends up living with the handler."

🐾 *Some people have the notion that a savage dog makes a good guard dog. In fact, security dogs need a friendly, trusting relationship with their handlers. Ron Minion's top dog, Romeo, adores Ron, and likes to hurl himself into Ron's arms — sometimes snatching his cap along the way. Ron says that when guards fail his dog-handling course, "it's usually because they're rough with the dogs. They're control types. They probably treat people badly too."*

How do the dogs respond to all this care and attention? Consider the time one of the guards got caught up in a labor dispute at a gold mine. He rolled down the window of his patrol truck to talk to the protesters, but they smashed the windshield with a rock, wounding him badly in the head. As he radioed for help, they tried to drag him out of the truck. The dog leapt into the fray, snarling and snapping, and held the attackers off, on all sides, until the guard was rescued.

Dogs lend us their protective services in curious ways. For example, in some small zoos that can't afford much security, they work alone to protect the residents. Foxes and coyotes – and, for that matter, human thieves – see certain caged animals as an easy meal. That's why, if you look past the deer and mountain goats pushing their noses against the fence, you may spot a dog moving from pen to pen, slipping through dog doors, overseeing your visit with a wary eye.

Then there's the fearless Karelian, from Finland. This midsized black-and-white spitz traditionally helped to hunt elk and bears. (Spitzes – such as huskies, chows, and Samoyeds – are adapted to the cold. They have thick coats, and small ears that won't easily freeze; often the furry tail curls up tightly over the rump. *Spitz* is German for "pointed," describing these dogs' fox-like muzzles.) These days, Karelians are protecting people from dangerous bears – and protecting the bears as well.

Here's the problem: as hikers and campers explore national parks and other wilderness areas, many black bears and grizzlies lose their fear of people – and gain a dangerous taste for groceries. Instead of killing these aggressive bears, or trapping them and moving them far from their homes, some wildlife specialists are hiring Karelians trained in *bear deterrence*. While their handlers shout and fire guns loaded with blanks, the Karelians face down the bears, snarling and snapping and barking and generally acting like the meanest set of teeth in the forest. Most bears take the hint, and learn to stay a safe distance from humans.

Born to Hunt

Although dogs and people have hunted together throughout history, the way they do it varies enormously. Is the prey large or small? Does it run, fly, or swim? Where is it found, and under what conditions? How many dogs are sharing the hunt, and how many humans? What weapons do they have? And what is the goal: fresh meat, amusement, trophies like skin or antlers, or simply the extermination of an unwelcome neighbor?

Over the years, many breeds of dog have been developed, and even named, for particular kinds of hunting. Cocker spaniels were bred to flush woodcocks. (Woodcocks are game birds. Flushing, or springing, means scaring prey out of the undergrowth and into the open.) Lymers, dogs who hunted on a leash – as bloodhounds do today – were called after an archaic word for "leash." Setters, pointers, springers, and retrievers are named for their behavior in the hunt. Most devious of all, tolling retrievers tease ducks from the shoreline, tempting the curious birds to swim nearer. ("Tolling" means "luring.") When the ducks are close enough, the hunters stand up and shoot them as they take flight. Many other dogs – including deerhounds, elkhounds, boarhounds, coonhounds, and otterhounds – bear the name of their prey.

For thousands of years, large animals like deer and wild boar were chased to exhaustion and either brought down by the dogs or cornered and killed by the

🐾 *A water spaniel flushes ducks along a shoreline. Spaniels may have originated in Spain and taken their name from* espagnol *(the French word meaning "Spanish").*

hunters, with clubs, spears, or bows and arrows. Small animals that lived above ground were flushed by dogs and trapped in nets. Birds were also flushed, sometimes into nets but sometimes into the sky, where a trained bird of prey – a hawk or falcon – was sent up to snatch them as they flew off.

Prey that lived underground – foxes, rabbits, badgers – were located by the long, stubby-legged dachshund – *Dachs* is German for "badger" – and by basset hounds and other low-slung dogs who could tunnel into the dens, digging furiously with sharp, back-curved claws.

Various kinds of terriers were also bred to pursue animals into the earth (*terra* is Latin for "earth"). They had to be persistent and fearless, since only a brave, relentless dog would plunge into a dark hole in search of prey. Many terriers have wiry coats that protect them from rocky tunnels, and from the teeth and claws of their frantic prey, and a piercing bark to let the hunters keep track of where the dogs are once they disappear beneath the ground. For a while, white terrier puppies were considered unlucky, and were drowned. But dark terriers were easily mistaken for prey, especially when they were coated with muck, so whiter breeds like the West Highland and the Jack Russell were developed.

Following the Hounds

The word "hound" is a general term for certain kinds of dogs who are natural hunters. Hounds often hunt in packs, and run down their prey with or without the help of people. Some lean, muscular dogs are known as "sight hounds" or "gaze hounds" because they spot their prey from a long way off, with their acute vision, and run it down. Others are "scent hounds" who track animals by their spoor (smell). Scent hounds can be either ground-scenters (like bloodhounds), who sniff the ground, or air-scenters (like foxhounds), who catch the scent in the air. Treeing hounds are scent hounds who track tree-climbing animals such as raccoons.

When scent hounds in a pack catch the spoor, they bay (howl) to tell the others. When they can no longer follow the scent, they fall silent until they find it again. So a pack of scent hounds creates a chorus of baying, as various dogs catch and lose the spoor. As the pack closes in on the game, and more of the dogs can stay on the scent, the baying grows louder and more continuous.

The graceful, long-legged Saluki, so prized by Arab sheiks, is a hound who originally hunted in the deserts of the Middle East. All the members of the hunting party (including the Salukis) would travel into the desert by camel. A trained hawk might be sent up into the sky to find some prey – an antelope, say – and the Saluki would run the beast down, at speeds of forty miles (over 60 km) an hour or more. The Saluki could also maneuver quickly, keeping pace as the frantic antelope dodged and swerved. Hard pads on the dog's feet protected them from the blistering heat of the sand.

On the steppes (plains) of Russia, the Mongols despatched borzois – also hounds – in teams of three, matched for size and speed. (In Russian, *borzyi* means "fast.") The team would chase down a wolf, surround it, and veer into it, knocking it over and holding it until the hunter arrived. In later years these tall, elegant dogs were prized by the aristocracy of the czars. Many were slaughtered during the Russian Revolution, as tokens of their owners' wealth and decadence.

🐾 *The pointer locates prey by smell, and freezes in an odd posture — like an arrow aimed at a target — with one forefoot raised. Then the dog begins to tremble, as if overwhelmed by anticipation. If two pointers are used, from different directions, the hunter can triangulate — that is, figure out where the paths of the two "arrows" would cross — to determine the prey's exact position.*

In Africa the basenji hunted in the tall, dry grass of the savannah. Basenjis are sometimes called jumping-up-and-down dogs, because they leap into the air to get a better view over the grass. Although these hounds can bark if they want to – or even howl like a Swiss yodeler – they almost never do; a quiet hunter is a well-fed hunter.

Gun Dogs

Several new categories of dog were developed after the late 1600s, when guns became accurate enough, and simple enough, to be used for hunting birds. Now a hunter needed a pointer, a dog who silently found the prey and pointed out its location and then *stayed still*, out of the line of fire, while the hunter went through the steps of loading his weapon and creeping close enough to shoot. As guns became more accurate and faster to load, another gun dog, the setter, was used; it would locate the prey, sit ("set") until the hunter was ready, and then sweep through the brush, swinging its tail from side to side, until the birds were flushed.

Retrievers were used when there were many hunters, or when a shot bird landed in water or marsh; they have an uncanny sense of precisely where a bird has fallen, and learn to pick it up gently and bring it back intact. Poodles are fine retrievers – they will even retrieve arrows – and they too retrieve from water. Their name comes from the German *Pudel*, or "puddle," and they are excellent swimmers. Their dense, curly coat helps keep them warm and dry in the water. The traditional poodle trim – with pompoms of hair around the chest and joints – was designed to keep their joints and vital organs warm, and to buoy them up in the water like a lifejacket.

Sturdy, thick-coated Japanese Akitas hunted bears and other large game, but they were also the synchronized swimmers of the canine world. They would ride out in fishing boats and, on command, jump into the water and swim in a row, driving fish into the waiting nets.

Dressed to Kill

In England, once the bears and wild boars were gone and deer had become scarce, a fashionable country-house lifestyle developed around foxhunting. In earlier years foxes had been regarded as useless pests, and routinely exterminated by farmers, but now such "vulpicide" was forbidden. Foxes were to be killed only for sport. Riders assembled in their trim black or bright red hunting jackets, tight white breeches, and

🐾 *Hunting for sport has long been controversial, defended by some and deplored by others. "Hunting I reckon very good / To brace the nerves and stir the blood," wrote one poet, while another called it "Detested sport, That owes its pleasure to another's pain." Whatever its merits or evils, sport hunting has led to the development of an astounding range of breeds.*

two-tone hunting boots, on specially bred hunters (horses). A large pack of hounds, chosen for their harmonious appearance and sound and trained by huntsmen, was set loose to sniff out a fox. When they flushed one and began the chase, horses and riders would charge after the pack, through crops and pastures and anything else in their path. The whole operation was commanded by a Master of Foxhounds – often a wealthy landowner, even a nobleman. Between hunts there were hunt club dinners and hunt club balls. The sport was celebrated in poems, novels, and drawings, and the country's most famous painters did grand portraits of favorite horses and hounds. Eventually, foxes became so rare that they had to be smuggled in from other regions – or even other countries – and the foxhunt began to decline.

The Inner Dog

Why are certain dogs so good at working with people? Why are different dogs better at different tasks? Some experts divide canine intelligence into three categories: instinctive, adaptive, and working.

Instinctive intelligence includes the tendencies that dogs inherit through their genes: to bark or not bark, hunt or not hunt, retrieve or not retrieve, and so on. We can affect these tendencies over generations of breeding, but we can't do much to change them in an individual dog. Barkers want to bark, hunters want to hunt, retrievers want to retrieve.

Adaptive intelligence is the ability to solve problems and learn new skills. Dogs with a lot of adaptive intelligence are good at dealing with unfamiliar situations, and either changing the situation or changing their behavior to deal with it. High instinctive intelligence and high adaptive intelligence tend not to go together.

Working intelligence is the ability to obey a leader. To have a high working intelligence, dogs first need a strong desire to please (*Okay, boss, what do you want?*). Since we can't really tell them what we want, these dogs also have a knack for understanding us (*I guess you want me to do something with this ball – but what?*), the ability to keep concentrating in spite of distractions (*Oh, you don't want me to bring it? Okay, let's try something else*), and the flexibility to think of new answers (*How about if I put the ball in the box? Oh, so THAT'S what you wanted! . . . Now can I have a biscuit?*).

Dogged Statistics

Scientists have studied the instinctive behavior of dogs in considerable detail. One study measured thirteen tendencies in fifty-six breeds. This is how four breeds ranked, out of a maximum score of 100:

	Golden Retriever	Standard Poodle	Basset Hound	Miniature Schnauzer
obedience training	90	100	10	7
playfulness	90	40	10	100
defending the home	40	10	10	100
destructiveness	10	40	20	80
excessive barking	10	50	40	100

Which are the best characteristics? That depends on what you're looking for.

If all this sounds too theoretical, ask yourself: if you were choosing a police dog, would you pick one who follows instructions, or one with a strong instinct to chase small animals? If you were blind and you were choosing a dog to lead you, would you pick one who depends on instructions, or one who can deal with the unexpected? All three forms of intelligence are valuable, but the dog has to be right for the job.

Dogs in Sheep's Clothing

When dogs have the job of guarding other large animals – a flock of sheep, a herd of cows or reindeer – they get along with them much the way a wolf might get along with its own pack. Often these dogs are raised with the flock from puppyhood, so they accept the flock as their family, and vice versa. Some breeds, like the maremma and the Pyrenean mountain dog, have been bred to be large, white, and woolly. The komondor has such a heavy white coat that it's shorn along with the flock it guards. The sheeplike look of these dogs is reassuring to the flock, and provides a nasty surprise for any predator that ventures into their midst.

A border collie shows "eye" as it stalks sheep and prepares to herd them. Althought this makes the sheep bunch together and move aways from the dog, these sheep seem to understand that he's no real danger; he's just a bossy supervisor telling them where to go and what to do.

Guard dogs and fighting dogs who had lighter, less protective coats were vulnerable to attackers, who might sink their teeth into an exposed ear or tail. That's why it became customary to amputate the earflaps and tails of some breeds. The practice continues today: a Doberman's ears may be lopped (trimmed to stand upright) to make the dog look more alert and fierce; the tail of a boxer or a Rottweiler may be docked (cut to leave just a stub) as a matter of fashion.

Dogs who actually herd the flock, moving it from place to place, are more like hunting dogs. They may cooperate with people, following spoken commands, hand signals, or just whistles, or the dogs may work alone. They keep the animals together and drive them in the desired direction; they round up any animals that break free. They may chase and stalk a wandering animal, crouching low and fixing it with a "strong eye" – like the pointer's fixed stare – to intimidate it. They may bark sharply and insistently to drive the animal back into the flock. Their mock hunting behavior is very similar to the way their ancestors cornered bears and wolves for the kill.

In New Zealand, it's not uncommon to find a few dogs caring for a huge flock of sheep. With or without human direction, the dogs maneuver to move the flock and keep it together. These dogs grow up with the flock, and they develop an extraordinary ability to see what's coming next,

> understanding that if a sheep looks in a certain direction, it is likely to go that way, and that the sheep are very stubborn animals. The heading or mustering dog also watches the shepherd, or boss, when he is present. If the boss levels his binoculars in a certain direction, the dog looks for action in that direction, and is ready to go.

As with hunting, techniques of herding and guarding depend on the circumstances. For example, in an area menaced by coyotes, the sheep may want to stay together for safety. A dog who can mingle with them, looking and acting like a

🐾 *Like the white komondor, the puli originally came from Hungary, and has a woolly coat that hangs in heavy cords, protecting the dog from enemies and bad weather. Although these dogs are usually black, they too are talented herding dogs, famous for their energy and agility. They sometimes run across the backs of the flock to reach a straying sheep. They may even stand on the wandering sheep's back, like a circus performer, and ride it in the right direction.*

sheep, is well placed to defend the whole flock. If the dog acted like a predator, the sheep would be frightened away. Once they were scattered, the smaller, weaker ones would soon be picked off by the coyotes.

But if the flock is widely spread out – perhaps in a region where grazing is scarce – the dog needs to be able to collect the animals quickly, moving them away or scaring them into a huddle until any danger is past. In this case, a dog who looks and acts threatening will have more power to protect the flock.

Dogs can herd cattle, too. How can they round up animals so much bigger than themselves? Sometimes by provoking the steer and then running in the desired direction, tricking the steer into pursuing them; sometimes by running straight at the animal, nipping its heels or even seizing it by the throat to force it back. With intelligence and daring, they get the job done, but it can be dangerous work. Some dogs learn to do a quick back-flip to avoid being kicked by a flailing hoof.

Traffic Wardens

Traditional jobs like herding can be useful in quite unexpected places. For example, geese and other large birds are a danger to airplanes, especially during takeoff and landing. The birds learn to ignore firecrackers and other tricks we use to scare them away. But if border collies patrol the airfield, chasing the birds off every time they try to settle, the birds soon move on – and nobody gets hurt.

Golf courses have a similar problem: geese move in and litter the pristine grass of the greens and fairways with messy, germ-laden droppings. Once they start nesting, the geese can be aggressive and intimidating. Border collies and other herding dogs work diligently, rain or shine, to keep the geese away. Since barking would disturb the golfers, the dogs simply fix the trespassers with a strong eye, and the geese look for another stopover. (The greenskeepers say that if the dogs were any smarter, they'd be driving golf carts.)

Dogs of Ice and Snow

While technology replaced dogpower in most of the developed world, in the Far North dogs were still pulling sleds and toboggans. The Inuit people of North America had been using dogs – especially spitzes – hundreds of years before the

Europeans arrived. A team of dogs would pull a komatik (sled) riding on long runners. The runners were coated with smooth, slippery mud to make them slide easily; once the mud froze, it was brushed with layer after layer of water, to build up a crust of ice. As the friction of the day's travel wore off the ice, it was simple to brush on a new coat.

As well as carrying and pulling loads for the Inuit, the dogs ran down wolves, caribou, muskox, and even polar bears, and held them until the men arrived with harpoons. For the seal hunt, they sniffed out the snow-covered holes in the ice where the seals came up to breathe and led the hunters there to wait.

In Siberia, in Russia's Far North, Samoyed dogs pulled sleds and herded reindeer. Here, as in North America, dog hair was sometimes used to make warm clothing. The dogs of Lapland, in northern Scandinavia, herded reindeer for human herders who traveled on skis.

With their dense coats, the thick-coated spitzes can survive frigid weather that would kill most pack animals. Sled dogs can sleep outdoors through an Arctic night, and wake up the next morning to shake off the snowdrifts and go back to work. Fur between their toes protects their feet from freezing. (It also spreads their body weight over the top of the snow – as if they were wearing little snowshoes – so they don't fall through.) On especially cold nights, though, the dogs may be allowed to sleep indoors.

Most sled dogs are less than domesticated, and tend to be independent; they don't identify closely with their human partners. After all, the dogs work as a team, and they live almost entirely outdoors. Also, from time to time they interbreed with wolves. This brings healthy wild blood and new stamina into the breed, but it also brings a wilder heritage, creating dogs who are less bonded to their human families.

Sled dogs were especially useful during the 1800s and early 1900s, when Europeans were buying more and more furs from America. Organizations like the Hudson's Bay Company sent agents into the North to buy great quantities of pelts from hunters and trappers, and to set up trading posts where pelts could be exchanged for food and other goods. The managers of the trading posts bought dogs from the Inuit to guard the posts and the valuable merchandise, and to transport loads in and out of the wilderness. A team of four or five "freighting dogs" could be harnessed together to pull a sled piled high with furs and trade goods. The teams were especially useful in deep snow, because dogs were light enough to run across the top of the brittle crust, where a horse or mule would fall through.

Dick Bonnycastle, an employee of the Hudson's Bay Company in the 1920s, found out first-hand how stubborn and mischievous sled dogs could be. He and two colleagues, Conn and Angus, hitched a company dog team to a toboggan to practice running the dogs. As it turned out, it was the dogs who ran the men:

> Conn was left behind and I tripped and fell, still hanging on to the trailing-rope. I was dragged a bit before it was pulled out of my hands and the dogs careered up the beach dragging the empty toboggan. I caught them after a half-mile run. Angus arrived, we turned them around and came back at a tremendous pace. We tried to stop them near Conn: I stuck out my leg and almost got it twisted out of joint. It is impossible to hold back seven dogs with an empty toboggan when they want to go.

A few days later, Bonnycastle dared to take the dogs out on a short trip:

> They started fighting and trying to beat it into the bush. We went a mile or two but it was heavy going so I turned them around and in doing so dropped the whip. I tied the toboggan to a tree stump while I retrieved my whip. When my back was turned they jumped and the rope came off the stump and they were away. I tore after them all the way home. . . .

Pole to Pole

In the early 1900s, explorers ventured farther and farther into polar lands, seeking the glory of reaching the North and South poles. Sled dogs played a vital role in these expeditions, but they paid a terrible price. Some died of disease, injury, or exhaustion. Some froze to death. Since meat was scarce, weaker dogs were killed and their bodies were fed to the rest of the pack.

Robert E. Peary, an American, claimed to have reached the North Pole in 1909, but most of his 133 dogs died along the way. Roald Amundsen, a Norwegian, had 92

🐾 *Panikpah, one of Robert Peary's dogs, survived terrible hardships in the Arctic, once going without food for two weeks. Although sled dogs were often killed when they were no longer useful, Panikpah remained the explorer's dear friend. "It is a waste of meat to feed him," declared Peary, "yet he shall be fed until he dies, for his splendid work in the past."*

dogs when he set off into Antarctica, but only 18 were still alive when he reached the South Pole in 1911.

Dogs returned to Antarctica in the 1940s, to pull sleds for the scientists working there, but they were gradually replaced by snowmobiles. In the 1990s all non-native animals (except humans) were banned from Antarctica, to protect the natural environment there; a few remaining dogs were sent to the other end of the planet, to their ancestors' Arctic home.

Today, most of the traditional jobs of Arctic dog teams have been taken over by vehicles. But dogs remain in the north as pets, dogsled racing is increasingly popular as a sport (see Chapter Eight), and dogsledding is becoming a tourist attraction. One way or another, these hardy dogs may be racing over ice and snow for years to come.

CHAPTER FOUR

Making Sense of Scents

When Ron Minion was with the Royal Canadian Mounted Police, he and his dog Sheba were called to a burgled office building, late at night. While Sheba tracked the burglar's scent out of the building, Ron followed her through the darkness by flashlight. Before long, he heard Sheba's teeth click on something; she had found a small, ring-shaped piece of gold. Next, she found a little glass disk. But this mysterious trail ran out at the roadside; the thief must have used a getaway car.

Later, at the police station, Ron saw a man who'd been stopped for a traffic offense, and he noticed that the front of the man's watch was damaged; the gold bezel and the glass crystal were gone. Sheba's amazing nose had found the missing parts – and Ron had found his burglar.

Dogs clearly enjoy their keen sense of smell; they revel in the scent of every dead beetle, every wad of old chewing-gum. An open door brings a host of new aromas to tickle their noses, and a fresh breeze carries more messages than a mail truck.

Why can they smell things so much better than we can? Dog experts aren't absolutely sure, but the answer seems to be something like this. High up in your own nose, there's an area of less than one and a half square inches (about 9 cm²) that's covered with a special *olfactory membrane.* ("Olfactory" means related to the sense of smell.) This membrane is larger than the area it covers, because it's gathered into folds, instead of lying flat. It's covered with olfactory cells, and they don't lie flat either; each one branches out into tiny, hairlike arms called cilia. So the surface area we use for smelling – including all the cilia on all the cells on all the folds of the membrane – is more than you might expect in our short little noses. The scent messages those cells pick up are passed along your nerves to be analyzed by an olfactory bulb in your brain.

A dog's olfactory membrane lies over a fine, intricately folded bone structure. Depending on the breed and size, the membrane may be anything from under three square inches to over twenty-three square inches (18 to 150 cm²) – in other words, anything from twice as large as ours to *fifty times as large.* If you could flatten out all those folds and cilia, the membrane would be big enough to cover the whole outside of the dog's body.

Here's how it works. The dog's moist nose captures the odor, and it's passed to the olfactory membrane. The odor gets caught in the tiny folds of the membrane, giving the olfactory cells lots of time to translate the smell into the message that goes to the olfactory bulb. The olfactory bulb is also larger, in proportion, than ours. (Some types of scents may be processed in a different way: captured by the *vomeronasal organ,* above the roof of the mouth, and passed to other parts of the brain.)

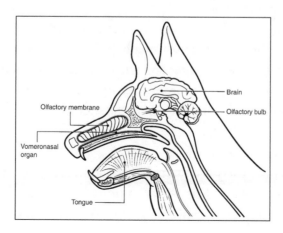

But there's more to it than that. Because most smells weren't all that important to our ancestors, our brains have a strong *suppression mechanism* that encourages us to ignore odors, and concentrate instead on sights and sounds and other things that matter more to us. But since many dogs were deliberately bred for their sense of smell, they have a weak suppression mechanism; their brains have evolved to focus on odors.

What does that mean, in practical terms? It means that, in scientific studies, some dogs seem to be able to detect certain odors that are a *million times weaker* than the level we can detect. It means that a dog with a good nose can pick out your smell – and can tell it from the smell of your brother or sister – and can smell the difference between twins, even if they grew from the same cell and they're identical right down to their DNA.

What's so smelly about people? First of all, there's our sweat, which carries a mixture of our body chemicals. We tend to sweat more in our armpits and our groins, which is why dogs love to sniff these parts of our bodies. There are also our dead skin cells. About fifty million skin cells flake off our bodies every day, to be replaced by new cells. We leave a trail of these old cells behind us, wafting through the air, swirling on the breeze, drifting to the ground – rather the way smoke spreads from a small fire. The dead cells and the bacteria they carry create a trail, and nobody's trail smells exactly the same as someone else's. On top of that, of course, there are all the smells from the food we eat, the places we go, the clothes we wear, the toiletries we use, and so on.

An odor is strongest right near the source and gets weaker as you move away, so a dog tracks an odor by following its strength. If the odor gets weaker, the dog stops and *casts about*, trying to find a direction where it's stronger. You can think of this pattern as a *scent cone*, with the source of the odor at the pointed end of the cone, and the dog at the broad end, homing in on the source.

A Nose Is Not Enough

It takes more than just nose-power to make a good working dog. We need dogs who are focused and attentive – dogs who can ignore a smorgasbord of fascinating odors, and apply themselves to specific smells. We need dogs who can resist that flash of squirrel running by, those car horns and sirens, that half-eaten cheese sandwich lying on the ground – dogs who will, if necessary, crawl into dark, cramped, even dangerous places, and go on working when they're tired and hungry.

Why do some dogs give us all this effort and self-control, often on a mission they don't understand? Because they have been trained, patiently and thoughtfully, by experts who understand how a dog's mind works, and how much a dog can and cannot do. Through months of training, and ongoing practice and retraining throughout their working lives, the dogs' own instincts and desires are directed toward the jobs we need them to do.

Schooldays

Although the Royal Canadian Mounted Police – the RCMP, or Mounties – are famous for their horses, they also have a long tradition of canine partners. These days, the RCMP have about 120 dogs. Most are male and most are German shepherds, because these dogs have the agility and assertiveness for general police work, but some Labrador retrievers work in the units policing the illegal drug trade. About half the dogs are bought from outside sources when they're a year or two old, and the rest are bred by the RCMP.

🐾 An RCMP dogmaster and sled dog. The RCMP have been Canada's national police force for more than eighty years, enforcing the law over vast areas of wilderness. In the past, dogs provided transportation as well as protection and good company. These days the Mounties no longer patrol by dogsled, but their dogs are valuable partners in many other ways.

Speaking of Training . . .

The RCMP is a good example of training because the Mounties prepare dogs for jobs in a number of government departments, and they have many years of practice. But every training organization has its own methods and vocabulary. Some police dogs and handlers are called canine (or K-9) units; others are known as PDS (Police Dog Services). Some organizations say their detector dogs "alert" when they find the right smell; others say their dogs "indicate." That's why this book sometimes uses one word, and sometimes another.

Before dogs begin the RCMP training program, they are carefully assessed for health, temperament, and "retrieve drive" – that is, their determination to follow a scent no matter how difficult it gets. The dogs have to be gentle enough to be trusted with schoolchildren, yet aggressive enough to defend their human partners if necessary.

Except for the Labs, all RCMP dogs learn general police-dog skills. Over the course of their training, they master a number of profiles (areas of expertise), including obedience, agility, tracking, retrieval, criminal apprehension, searching buildings and alleys, and finding firearms, small articles, and missing persons. Most of the dogs are taught drug detection, but some learn explosives detection instead.

Let's follow an imaginary dog and handler – we'll call them Thumper and Alex – through their schooling. The two meet at the Police Dog Services training center in western Canada, and start by getting acquainted: playing, taking long walks, and bonding as a team.

The first stage of Alex and Thumper's training, Level One, usually lasts about five weeks. For obedience training, the team practices basic spoken commands such as sit, heel, down, and right and left turns, with Thumper on a leash most of the time. For criminal apprehension, Thumper learns to bite a padded sleeve worn by another handler, and to hold on until Alex says to let go. While Thumper learns what all the commands mean, Alex is learning how to teach this particular dog – because no two dogs are the same – and how to correct mistakes without losing Thumper's trust. The dogs are never physically punished, and never trained to the point of frustration. They are praised and rewarded, or corrected and sent back to try again; on occasion, if they are performing very poorly, they are scolded, but nothing more. Teamwork is based on trust. Physical abuse and trust don't go together.

Alex also leads Thumper through a demanding course of agility training. Thumper learns to clamber up one side of an obstacle and skitter down the other, and to make his way across a long, slippery log or a swaying wooden bridge. This is good practice for police work, and it helps Thumper develop strong muscles, and better balance and agility. It also builds his self-confidence and his trust in Alex. But don't think Thumper is doing all the work. When the dog falls off that slippery log, or misses a step and tumbles head over heels, Alex is there to catch him and hoist him back up.

🐾 *RCMP Corporal Dave Koekman helps Rex scramble over a stack of oil barrels as part of his agility training. Dave has had two narcotics-detecting dogs – first Ben, then Max – but now his city needs an explosives dog, so Max has been reteamed with another handler, and Dave and Rex are learning the explosives profile. Reteaming is unusual; most dogs stay with their first partners.*

The most time-consuming part of Level One is tracking, which is now the main job of RCMP Police Dog Services (PDS). Whether a small child is lost in a forest or an armed convict is on the run, the skills of the PDS team can make the difference between life and death.

Ron Minion still remembers the time a five-year-old named Bonnie wandered away from her family's ranch in winter. Fifty construction workers from a nearby plant joined the search for the child, but no one could find her. The parents were desperate; it was a freezing night, and there were bears around.

The very cold weather made it impossible for Sheba to follow Bonnie's trail, but Ron set the dog loose on a free-ranging search to see what she could turn up. For hours he followed the dog by flashlight. At four o'clock in the morning, when Sheba finally found the little girl lying motionless on the ground in her flimsy overalls and jacket, Ron feared the worst. But Bonnie woke up when Sheba licked her face, and Ron carried the child home to her family.

As for Thumper, he starts by learning to track on a leash, leading Alex along a scent trail. First, somebody (called the quarry) lays a track for the dog by taking a long and complicated walk – along roads, up hills and down valleys, across fences and bridges, through fields and trees, sometimes doubling back to make a dead end in the trail. From time to time, the quarry drops a small piece of cloth to encourage the dog. (People who work as quarry sleep with these scraps of cloth in their beds, to get them loaded with body scent.) The quarry then chooses a hiding place at the far end of the trail.

Some time later – when the scent trail has had time to age and wear off a little – Alex and Thumper set off to follow it, and the training officer goes with them. Thumper finds the scent and tracks it, ground-scenting. If he starts air-scenting, Alex corrects him. If Thumper loses the scent, Alex guides him in circles to find it again. (Alex will see the *head snap* as Thumper locks onto the scent and gets back to work.) If Thumper *stops to mark* (urinates) or *goes to animal* (is distracted, perhaps by the smell of a squirrel or rabbit), or just loses interest, Alex reminds him to "soo" (seek).

Meanwhile, the training officer is watching their every move, noting how efficiently both Thumper and Alex do their jobs. If they lose the track entirely – remember, Alex doesn't know where it goes either – the trainer will help them get started again. When Thumper finally finds the quarry at the end of the trail, he's rewarded with hugs and praise and a few moments of play with his favorite ball.

During Level One, the tracking exercises slowly get longer and more difficult, and the tracks are aged more and more before the team is allowed to start. When they move on to Level Two, for another three to six weeks, the trails are laid through busier areas, with more distractions and confusing smells, and the dog learns to search buildings. Obedience training moves *off line* – Thumper is no longer on a leash – and Alex begins using hand signals as well as voice commands. Thumper has to locate the kind of evidence real quarry might lose or discard – gloves, a purse, a gun. He also learns criminal apprehension off line – that is, Alex drops the leash and sends Thumper to chase down the suspect.

Level Three takes yet another three to five weeks. Alex and Thumper work on tracking in busy parts of the city, through traffic and the powerful smells of people and other dogs and food and garbage. Obedience training is off line and depends on

🐾 *Training Sergeant Pete Nazaroff watches closely as two of his students follow a scent trail across the countryside. "When a dog isn't working successfully, we look for our mistakes first, and whether we're handling the dog right," he says.*

🐾 *RCMP Corporal Chris Lohnes wears a padded sleeve so that Dasty can practice using his teeth to seize a fugitive and hold on until he's called off. Most police forces teach their dogs to stop a suspect this way. A few teach the more difficult technique of "bark and hold," in which the dog corners the suspect with ferocious barking and bites only if the person refuses to stop.*

hand signals alone. The dogs learn their specialties – detecting eight different illegal drugs or twenty-two different explosives. No dog learns both drugs and explosives. Training Sergeant Pete Nazaroff says there's a good reason: "If we're out there looking for a bomb, we don't want the dog confused by some bystander who smells of marijuana."

During the course of all this training, Thumper is gradually exposed to more upsetting distractions, such as gunfire and – of course – horses. Meanwhile, Alex is brushing up on canine first aid and CPR, in case Thumper ever gets hurt. Alex will always carry first-aid supplies like splints and bandages, as well as an antidote to narcotics, in case the dog swallows some, and an emetic (to make him vomit) in case he swallows poison.

At the end of Level Three the successful teams graduate, but their training is far from over. They will work through Level Four on their own, refining and strengthening their skills. After they graduate, the two partners have to be retested every year to be sure they remember all their lessons. They even have post-graduate courses in special subjects. For example, some dogs are specially trained in crowd control; protected by vests like the body armor their handlers wear, they can help defend a person or a building. (Dog vests haven't been used much except for crowd control – they've been too heavy and hot, limiting the dog's performance – but better vests are being designed.)

Despite everyone's best efforts, many of the dogs who enter Level One never graduate; they just can't meet the RCMP's standards. Most of them end up working as guard dogs, or in similar roles that don't need such a high level of discipline and training. As for their handlers, they say a sad goodbye to this partner of many weeks, and bond with a new dog and start back at the beginning.

Trainers and Handlers

Pete Nazaroff has been a Mountie for twenty-four years, and he's been in PDS for fourteen years. Now that he's a training sergeant, he teaches other handlers how to work with new dogs, and how to understand them and trust them. "We have to believe our dogs," he says. "Our dogs don't lie to us." But he also knows that even the best-trained dog is still a dog.

"I remember working a murder scene out in the bush, with my dog Brutus, a German shepherd," he says. "Brutus was searching off line and suddenly he came tearing back, and his eyes were like saucers. I went to welcome him – I figured either he'd found something or he really wanted to play – but he blasted right by me and kept going. That's when I saw the big black bear coming right behind him!"

Being a police-dog handler is a rewarding job, but it's also a very demanding one. Training with a new dog means spending months away from home. After graduation, the teams are on call at all hours – they may be needed in the middle of the night, perhaps for many hours of scrambling over rough country, never knowing what dangers lie ahead. RCMP dogs live with their handlers, and they need lots of exercise every day, and practice in all their skills. Once a year, both the dog and the handler have to pass another medical and physical exam, and go through further training and testing.

One of Pete Nazaroff's students, Corporal David Hansen, already has a narcotics dog, a Malinois named Buck. (A Malinois is the Belgian equivalent of a German shepherd.) David's region needs an explosives dog as well, so he's now doing the explosives profile with Astro. He'll have his hands full with two dogs to work and exercise and retrain. On top of that, there's the question of how well Astro and Buck will get along with each other.

"Buck is a real character," says David. "Among other things, he's crazy about stuffed animals. We once did a demonstration at an overnight youth rally, and I wanted to show off Buck's obedience skills, so I put him in the down position and

❧ RCMP dog Tuff scales a board wall eight feet (2.5 m) high. Agility is vital for a police dog; wherever a suspect flees, the dog has to follow. Courage is also essential; even if the suspect starts shooting, the dog will keep up the chase.

walked away. The kids started laughing. When I looked around, Buck was crouching just the way he should be. I looked away and they laughed; I looked back and he was fine. It turned out that whenever I wasn't watching, Buck was sprawling on his back and waving his legs in the air. So much for obedience! I decided to move on to retrieving, but Buck beat me to it – I turned my back for a second, and he buried his head in a student's duffel bag and retrieved her stuffed Dalmatian!"

Where do the handlers come from? RCMP officers who want to become handlers have to show their talent and dedication by helping the trainers in their spare time, without pay. They may raise puppies for the program, or lay scent tracks, or assist in other ways. Despite the joys of the work, many handlers transfer out of the program when their first dog retires. They find that it's just too stressful and time-consuming, and adds too many complications to their private lives.

Specialty #1: Narcotics Detecting

The international trade in illegal drugs is a vicious business. The criminals who run the drug cartels enjoy lives of luxury, while the sleazy work of smuggling and selling the drugs is carried out by addicts and other people who will do just about anything to make a few dollars.

Because even a small shipment of illegal drugs can sell for a lot of money, dealers and smugglers go to great effort and expense to hide their wares. They seal drugs inside furniture, vacuum-pack them in cans, stuff them into tangerines, submerge them in automobile gas-tanks, coat them with chocolate, or bury them in strong-smelling products like pepper or coffee.

In one case, a German pointer named Bo crawled under a Volkswagen bus and chewed at the oilpan; two million dollars' worth of heroin was found in a false compartment beside the engine. In another case, 125 pounds (57 kg) of heroin was sealed into almost two thousand imitation duck eggs, and the fake eggs were mixed in with hundreds of thousands of real duck eggs. Did the heroin get past the dogs? Not a chance.

But some odors are harder to identify than others. If the dog is unsure because the scent is weak or confusing, the handler may move on to the next suitcase or the next passenger without giving the dog time to decide. If the smell is too strong, the

🐾 *RCMP dog Max checks luggage on an airport carousel with his handler, Sergeant Dan Jean. Although dogs are the best tool we have for detecting hidden caches of illegal foods and drugs — and the only tools that can walk along a moving carousel — they're not infallible. Some legal products smell very similar to illegal ones. And because they don't understand the reason for the search, dogs sometimes try to take shortcuts. They may look for cues: if the handler doesn't seem suspicious of someone, the dog may be careless too. Or they may check for the wrong item; one dog was trained on drug samples in plastic bags, and began alerting for all plastic bags!*

dog may have trouble pointing out the source, because there's no clear scent cone; there's too much scent everywhere. That's why training and teamwork are so important; the handler has to interpret the dog's body language, and trust the dog's nose, even if the dog seems to be on the wrong track.

Dave Koekman remembers how much he trusted his first narcotics dog, Ben. "Ben and I were called in to search this big house. Ben indicated the bathroom cupboard, under the sink, so we searched the cupboard. There was nothing there. But Ben kept indicating the cupboard, and he wouldn't stop, so finally we pulled off the kickboard underneath. We found $100,000 worth of cocaine. What really made that special for me was that another team had searched that house two months earlier, but they didn't bother to call in a dog. And they didn't find anything."

We'll talk more about narcotics dogs in Chapter Five.

Specialty #2: Explosives Detecting

The Chinese invented gunpowder about 1,200 years ago. It was used in fireworks at first, and later in weapons. About 150 years ago we learned to use nitroglycerine — often mixed with something absorbent to make dynamite, which is safer to work with than gunpowder. Since then, we have developed other explosives that are more sophisticated and – unfortunately – easier to carry in secret.

We hear a lot about military explosives – grenades, bombs, missiles – but explosives have many commercial uses too. They help us build roads and canals and train lines and subways; they let us mine for minerals and demolish old buildings without damaging the surroundings. But because they are used for so many purposes – and because some explosives are easily made – terrorists and other criminals sometimes lay hands on them.

That's where dogs come into the story. If people are hiding illegal explosives, or trying to smuggle explosives across a border, an explosives-detecting dog is the most efficient way to catch them. If there are reports that a bomb has been planted, or if a major event is planned that might attract terrorists, dogs can quickly check out every corner and crevice of the location. And when there has been an explosion, these same dogs can search for clues to what caused it.

It's a tough job, because today's explosives come in many forms and colors. There are plastic explosives like C-4 and the Semtex compounds, popular with terrorists. (Semtex doesn't have a natural smell of its own, but a smell is added to make it easier to detect.) There are watery explosives and jelly-like ones. There is deta (detonator) sheet, an explosive plastic sheet that can be molded into innocent-looking shapes, and det cord, which looks like rope. A good explosives dog alerts to all of these, and more – and does it passively, without touching the suspicious object, to avoid accidentally setting off an explosion.

In explosives work, as in narcotics, the handler has to watch the dog closely. "Only he knows what he's smelling," says Detective Bob Noll, who used to run the K-9 program for the police bomb squad in New York. "You have to pay attention to him. You miss a bomb, and it lets you know."

RCMP Corporal Don Chenel has fond memories of his old German shepherd, Duke. In the course of his career, Duke tracked down lost people, car thieves, armed robbers, and drug smugglers. He raced through the bush, through branches that cut his nose and left his eyes bleeding, to catch escaped convicts and suspected rapists, and he discovered the grisly remains of several bodies.

🐾 *Duke keeps an eye on forty bottles of home-brewed alcohol that he found hidden in a barn, behind a false wall. Home brew (also called moonshine) is not only illegal but dangerous; if it's contaminated, it can leave the drinker sick, blind, or even dead.*

Unusually, Duke was also an expert explosives dog. In one case, he sniffed out explosives hidden on a dead body. In another, he was flown to the Far North to find evidence in a bombing that had killed nine miners; two people were convicted.

Duke is now happily retired, but Don still misses his old partner. "He was a great dog. It was very rarely that we didn't come out of the bush with the bad guy."

What If You See a Police Dog?

If you're ever invited to meet a police dog – perhaps at school, or at some public event – don't be shy about saying hello. Handlers are proud of their dogs, and they like to explain the work they do. You can ask about the special equipment they carry – perhaps a tracking harness, a play toy to reward the dog, a can of skunk repellent to drive off unwelcome visitors. Some handlers carry an emetic; if the dog eats something poisonous, a dab of this medication in his eye will make him vomit. (But most police dogs are too well trained to take food from strangers.)

If you happen to encounter a canine team on active police duty, however, *leave them alone.* If they're following a scent, or trying to find one, distracting either the dog or the handler – or contaminating the scent trail with your own smell – could help a dangerous criminal to escape. If the dog is pursuing someone and you get in the way, you may be mistaken for the suspect. Besides, you don't know who the dog is after, or why; the situation may be far more dangerous than you imagine. Every year, police dogs are injured on the job – and some lose their lives.

The mood was somber that September day, as Pete Nazaroff supervised four dogs and handlers in their tracking practice. Pete's former dog, Vulcan, had just been gunned down, shot three times in the head and neck. Everyone was thinking about Vulcan – and about these dogs, who would face the same risks. Fortunately, Vulcan recovered from surgery, and he's now back on the job.

Not all police dogs are so lucky. In 1997, one Florida police corporal, Robin Massey, and her partner, Ralph, a Belgian Malinois, were chasing a robbery suspect. When the suspect jumped into a lake, Ralph jumped in after him and seized the man's shoulder. The man got a grip on Ralph and held him under the water until he drowned. Robin and four other officers jumped in to stop the man and rescue the dog, but it was too late.

Three hundred police officers and a hundred police dogs attended Ralph's memorial service. "You have to understand how cops feel," said one. "This is another cop. This is not just your dog; this is your partner." A twenty-one-gun salute was fired. A bugler played taps and a bagpiper played "Amazing Grace." A helicopter flew overhead bearing memorial wreaths.

One of the wreaths was shaped like a giant bone.

CHAPTER FIVE

The Nose Knows

One day, Pilot and I were screening airline passengers and he suddenly got really excited – like "Wow, I smell millions of dollars!" It turned out the passenger was a waitress going on holiday, and she had all her tips in her pocket. She was carrying hundreds of one-dollar bills. All U.S. bills are printed with the same ink, whether they're one dollar or a thousand dollars, so Pilot couldn't tell how much her wad of money was worth. He just knew it was a whole lot of bills.

– David Bailey, U.S. Customs agent

Pilot is eighteen months old. He's unusually big for a yellow Lab, but he still has an endearing puppy face. When he was little, he was used for research at a university. "It was humane stuff," says his handler, David Bailey, "but they were dabbing things on his skin to see if he reacted, things like that. When he got older he was put in a training program to be a leader dog for someone blind, but he was too wound up for that kind of work, so he came to U.S. Customs instead."

David supervises five Customs K-9 teams in Detroit, covering the main airport as well as seaports, bridges, and land borders. Although Customs has about 650 dogs, only 26 are trained to sniff out large amounts of paper money leaving the country.

David and Pilot often work in jetways, those tunnels you walk through to get from the air terminal to the plane. It's obvious when Pilot gets a whiff of something suspicious: he turns his head to get a better smell, his ears come up, his tail wags, and he leads David to the source and sits.

"It's not illegal to take money out of the U.S.," explains David. "But if you're taking more than $10,000, we need to report that to the Treasury. We need to make sure the money doesn't come from the drug trade, or some other international crime." In 2001, a dog in Miami caught $9 million being sent to the drug trade in Colombia; the money was tucked inside TV sets.

"These days, especially, we need to be sure it's not terrorist money. If you tell us you're carrying a lot of money, we check it out and you keep the money. But if you lie about the money and Pilot finds it, we have the right to take it away, and you may have a hard time getting it back."

Currency training is much like narcotics training. The U.S. Treasury sends Customs samples of the ink used to print money so the dogs can learn what they're looking for. "The dog has a rolled-up towel to play with – to play fetch and

The Business That Stinks

How do you train dogs to find explosives without storing a pile of things that go boom? How do you practice narcotics detection without a bagful of illegal drugs? Worse yet – what about those dogs who find decaying bodies?

One answer is pseudo scents: imitation scents that smell like specific drugs, or explosives, or corpses. Corpse scent comes in two flavors: dead less than a month, and dead for a long time. "Pseudo drowning victim" comes in a capsule you drop into water; the smell rises and forms a film on the water's surface. There's even "pseudo distressed body," which smells like somebody who is hurt and frightened but still alive.

Some trainers worry that dogs trained on fakes won't recognize the real thing. Police dogs train on real smells at least part of the time, so their scent-recognition will be accepted by the courts as a reliable indication of crime. Still, these little bottles are a lot handier than a cupboard full of dynamite, cocaine, and old body parts.

tug-of-war. We start by scenting the towel, with ink or marijuana or whatever, and the dog goes after the scent to find the towel – it's a new game. Then slowly we remove the towel from the equation, so the dog goes after the scent but the towel is still in the dog's mind – so if he smells narcotics in a car glovebox, he thinks, 'Oh boy, my towel's in there,' and he gets all excited and alerts."

Although narcotics dogs are tested using real drugs, they may do some of their training on pseudo scents. Customs handlers get real marijuana and hashish, but they use pseudo cocaine and heroin; it's safer for the dogs. Supervisors get real cocaine and heroin, as well as methamphetamines and ecstasy. Narcotics dogs learn to detect a lot of materials: cocaine base, crack, heroin base, Mexican brown heroin, China white heroin, and tar heroin, among others. As for Pilot, he gets to practice on real money. He has a play brick of eight hundred bills, shredded to bits and wrapped in plastic.

In the past, most Customs dogs were adopted from animal shelters, but these days Customs runs a puppy-breeding program. All the dogs go to school at the Canine Enforcement Training Center in Virginia, which Customs shares with the Bureau of Alcohol, Tobacco and Firearms (ATF). Dogs for other agencies – even other countries – are also trained there. After graduation, Customs dogs are retested every year, and judged on four points:

intent – how willing they are to work;
alert – how clear their response is to the scent;
interest – how keen they are to track the scent to its source;
response – whether they alert as they've been trained to, by sitting, scratching, or biting at the source of the scent.

Customs dogs live in kennels instead of with their handlers; it's simpler when there are so many of them, and it keeps the dogs excited about their job. They have lots of space and freedom at the kennels, but "work is the best fun they have," says David. The dogs retire when they're about seven years old – when they start losing interest – and either move in with the handler or go to an adopting family.

About sixty Customs dogs do passive response – they alert by sitting, which is good for a job like checking passengers lined up to board a plane, because it doesn't upset people. The rest do positive response – they'll try to follow the scent cone to its source, pawing or digging to reach it. They're great at searching buildings or vehicles. A K-9 team can go through a vehicle in five or six minutes, or check four or five hundred packages in half an hour.

"We work at the dogs' speed," says David. "They know their job, and they get used to all the strangers passing by, and the high frequencies of jet noise, which they hear a lot more acutely than we do. We send them into awkward spaces in ships and planes, and they crawl through small passages and climb over cargo – some of these dogs are like mountain goats; they'll climb almost anything. But we have to watch for hazards. For example, there's a lot of de-icing fluid around airplanes in winter, and it's poisonous. And in a warehouse there may be rat poison, or rat traps, or workers may be zooming around on forklifts.

"We catch people carrying illegal drugs in all kinds of places – taped to their skin, even stuffed inside the shoes on their feet. And when they're caught, they usually try to tell us they don't have anything. Some people seem to think it's okay to have these drugs if you have only a small amount. But when they buy anything from the drug trade, they make themselves part of that trade, and it's a vicious business. It kills people."

David used to have a golden retriever named Quaker, a narcotics dog trained for positive response. "He was positive, all right. One day I was in the baggage section of the airport, deep in discussion with another Customs agent. And a couple of postal workers wheeled a cart in, and the other agent said to me, 'What's your dog doing?' There was Quaker, chewing his way through the netting on the mail bag. We found two pounds of marijuana hidden inside.

"Quaker was a great dog, but he had a mind of his own. When he got tired or bored, he'd turn around and walk backwards – tail first, nose last. That was his way of saying, 'The nose is off the job.'"

Animal Trackers

After years of tracking animals for sport-hunters, dogs are now moving into the conservation business. The Pacific island of Guam has been called "the island where

❀ *USDA dog-handler Michelle Limtiaco directs Grommit, one of the snake-hunting Jack Russell terriers in Guam. With the help of tough little dogs like this, the birds will keep singing on other tropical islands.*

no birds sing," because brown tree snakes up to ten feet (3 m) long came in with cargo from Australia and elsewhere, and killed off most of the native birds. Now, Jack Russell terriers working for the U.S. Department of Agriculture (USDA) search airplanes and ships leaving Guam, and make short work of any brown tree snakes they find hitching a ride to other islands.

In marshy areas, dogs work with conservation officers to keep track of water-bird populations. They find birds' nests and flush the parent birds away so the eggs can be counted. They track down endangered birds for leg-banding or relocation to a safer place. In mountains and forests, dogs lead officers to various animals – from raccoons and lemmings to elk, moose, and mountain lions – so they can be immunized against disease, or marked or tagged for future identification. They find poachers, by sniffing out moose, bears, deer, and wild turkeys, as well as gunpowder. They spot birds and animals dying of disease or insecticide, or killed and abandoned by hunters, so authorities know how many animals are being lost this way.

In Africa, dogs are helping Kenya's park rangers track down poachers who slaughter elephants for their tusks and rhinoceroses for their horns. The dogs learned to sniff out ivory easily enough. It took them a little longer to get used to working around giraffes and warthogs.

In the state of Washington, scientists need to watch over endangered species such as the state's last twenty-odd grizzly bears. These giant bears are hard to find and dangerous to approach, but dogs can smell their scat (bear poop) from far off, and DNA analysis of discarded body cells in the scat identifies the bear it came from. Hormones in the scat of bears and other animals even tell us how stressed the animal is, by human disturbances or other pressures. Best of all, this long-distance testing doesn't add to the animals' stress.

There's at least one bearhound who works in reverse, starting on the bear's trail and tracking backwards to wherever the bear is coming from, so zoologists can check what the animal has been up to. Nobody's quite sure how the dog learned to do this, but it works.

In California, you can call out a tracking dog and a team of volunteers to search for a missing pet. Kat Albrecht, a retired police-dog trainer, heads a force of doggy detectives who track down lost dogs and cats – as well as horses, snakes, iguanas, ferrets, rats, hamsters, even a turtle. Since injured animals often crawl away and hide, finding them quickly may save their lives. And if it's too late – if the animal has been killed by a vehicle or a predator – Kat sends a cadaver dog to find the remains so the family can at least stop searching for their lost pet.

Here a Nose, There a Nose . . .

Termites do about two billion dollars' worth of damage to American houses every year, by chewing the wood out of walls and floors. It's hard for people to spot termites until the damage has been done, but dogs can sense them from the far side of a room, apparently by smelling chemicals produced by the insects' bodies. With training, the dogs learn exactly what they're looking for; they alert for many kinds of termites, but not for other insects such as cockroaches or carpenter ants, or for old tunnels that the termites have already abandoned.

There are dogs who sniff out the egg masses of gypsy moths; the leaf-eating larvae of these moths do immense harm to forests. Dogs learn to find patches of mold in lumberyards so the wood can be dried out and saved. Dogs spot moisture trapped in buildings, which causes mold and rot, or dry rot, a decay that turn wood into powder. Their noses also lead us to truffles, a gourmet fungus that grows underground. (Pigs can find truffles too, but they tend to gobble them up – and since truffles sell for hundreds of dollars a pound, they make expensive pigfood.)

We use underground pipelines to carry water, oil, natural gas, and certain chemicals. When a leak develops in a pipeline, not only is the fluid wasted, but it may pollute the ground. When technicians detect a drop in pressure in a stretch of pipeline, meaning that there is probably a leak, they can pump a special scent chemical into that section. Then detector dogs can travel over its path, hunting for the escaping chemical. One team of dogs pinpointed a leak in a northern Canadian pipeline buried under three feet (1 m) of snow and six feet (2 m) of frozen earth. Another team located twelve leaks beneath six feet of Louisiana swamp water and five feet (1.5 m) of mud; the dogs cruised over the pipeline in a boat and pawed the deck whenever they smelled the telltale chemical.

In Sweden, a German shepherd named Froy is checking universities and dental clinics for mercury. This liquid metal can enter our bodies through our skin, and it can poison us if we absorb too much. People sometimes discard mercury by dumping it down the drain. But it's heavy, so it collects in the U-bends of the plumbing, creating an environmental hazard. Without Froy, the Swedish Nature Protection Agency would have to open up a huge amount of plumbing. But the dog can tell which drains are contaminated, and he can check 250 drainpipes a day.

What about Froy's health? Kjell Avergren, the project leader, explains that mercury accumulates in the body over a lifetime; dogs just don't live long enough to collect a harmful level.

Dogs also do valuable detective work in the fight against arson. Suppose a business owner is losing money and burns down a warehouse to collect the insurance.

Or suppose someone wants revenge and sets fire to an enemy's house. Arsonists often think that if they start the blaze with gasoline or some other accelerant (very flammable material), the flames will destroy the evidence. But accelerant-detecting dogs can recognize traces of a dozen or more accelerants. When the dog alerts to something – maybe a section of blackened wall, or a patch of charred floorboard – the arson investigator takes a small sample for laboratory testing. If tests prove that accelerant was used, the "accidental fire" is investigated as a crime, and the motive and criminal are usually not hard to find.

Firefighter Chuck Geno works with Logan, a yellow Lab who was donated to the fire department in Dearborn, Michigan, by an insurance company. It makes good sense for insurance companies to sponsor arson dogs; the harder it is to disguise a deliberate fire as an accident, the less insurance money is paid for fraudulent claims. The very fact that a city employs an arson dog may discourage people from attempting this kind of fraud.

🐾 *Chuck and Logan on the scene of a double crime. A thief stole some guns from the house and started the fire in the hope of covering up the burglary. The house was damaged beyond repair, but Logan wasn't fooled a bit.*

Chuck remembers that as they investigated one house fire, the homeowner was watching Logan uneasily. "Is that one of those dogs who smell gasoline?" she asked the fire marshal.

"What do you think?" said the fire marshal.

"Did he find anything?" she asked.

"What do you think?" said the fire marshal.

"I started the fire myself!" the woman blurted – and Chuck looked down and saw that Logan was alerting to her clothes. Sure enough, her trousers and shoes tested positive for gasoline.

The Beagle Brigade

In 1984, the USDA set up a squad of beagles to patrol airports and postal centers, sniffing out meat and plant products that aren't allowed into the United States. Beagles were chosen partly because they are small, gentle, and cute – even cuter in their little green "Beagle Brigade" jackets – so passengers aren't alarmed as the dogs sniff their way past bags and suitcases, sitting down beside any bag that smells suspicious. The brigade now has over sixty teams of beagles and handlers. Other teams do a similar job in the Border Beagle Brigade, checking vehicles and baggage entering the United States from Canada and Mexico.

Becky Thormahlen used to be a Customs agent working with narcotics dogs. In 1999, she heard that the USDA was trying out a few larger dogs to inspect commercial cargo, since beagles weren't big enough to do some of the work. Becky left Customs and joined the USDA.

Her first partner there was Lori, a mix of black Lab and English setter who was "the best of the best," says Becky. "Almost perfect, except for her stubborn streak. She'd have driven the van if she could have, and I could have stayed home!" But Lori developed a health problem and moved to leisurely retirement. Becky got a new working partner, Tango, a pure black mostly-Lab from a rescue shelter.

"Tango started out as a slow learner," admits Becky. "She's full of enthusiasm, but sometimes she's exasperating because she just *doesn't get it* yet. Lori's attitude was, *I know my job, and I'll do it when I want to.* Tango's attitude is more like, *I'll do the job whenever you want, but – um – what am I supposed to do, again?* But she's still

🐾 *This USDA agent checks passengers from about seven flights a day. Every year the Beagle Brigade finds some 75,000 illegal items. The longer dogs are on the job, the more contraband they learn to recognize; some have mastered almost fifty different odors.*

very young, and she's starting to make some really good seizures. She's getting better all the time.

"When Tango came to me, she knew the basic odors she was looking for," says Becky. "But I had to teach her to search in the real world, in trucks and trains and warehouses and all kinds of boats, from ferries to private yachts. The two of us cover seven ports of entry. While Customs dogs are checking for drugs, Tango is looking for beef and pork, and all sorts of fruit – from apples and oranges to mango, kiwi, guava, avocado, lychee, and longan. She was taught to alert on some of these smells, and she generalized to the others; you might say she figured them out for herself."

Infected beef and pork can spread serious animal sicknesses like foot-and-mouth and mad-cow disease. Fruit can carry many diseases, funguses, and insects that could endanger crops in the U.S.A. One of the most dreaded pests is Med fly (Mediterranean fruit fly), which can lay waste to whole groves of citrus fruit.

But there's a big difference between agricultural work and narcotics work: most agricultural products are perfectly legal. Tango's world is full of orange juice and hamburgers and fruit salads. A bag that's full of books and newspapers today may have held someone's lunch yesterday. "It's her job to find the items," says Becky. "It's my job to decide if they're allowed into the country." When something is seized, there may be further testing by Becky and by the laboratory; any pests or diseases they find are reported so the USDA can keep track of these threats to agriculture.

Some people bring in meats and fruits innocently, not realizing that it's illegal. Some assume that anything legal in Canada must be legal in the United States; in fact, Canada admits tropical fruit more freely because, in the cold Canadian climate, there's no crop of these fruits to be put at risk. But other people knowingly smuggle in banned products just because they want them, in spite of the terrible damage they can do.

🐾 *Becky and Tango inspect the cargo in a tractor-trailer. Tango took her basic training in Florida, towering over her beagley colleagues like a colt among lambs. Until she retires, she can't live with Becky; the USDA, like U.S. Customs, boards its dogs in a kennel. "It's the Ritz-Carlton of kennels," says Becky, "but it's still a kennel."*

"I remember one family hiding longans in their car. They had these little fruits stuffed in their socks, in the kids' shoes, even in Mom's makeup bag. Another family tried to fool us by gift-wrapping every single piece of fruit. A lady traveling by bus thought she could sneak rambutans past us; when she was asked to get off the bus for inspection, she left the fruit on her bus seat, in a popcorn bag. I guess she thought nobody would look at popcorn. She was wrong! But maybe our easiest find was the man who hid ripe mangoes under the hood of his car, and practically baked them. We didn't need a dog to sniff out that one!"

What do people have to say for themselves when they've hidden illegal foods in ridiculous places, and lied to the officer, and been caught red-handed by a dog? "There's always some excuse," says Becky. "I guess my favorite is 'But that's not *food*. That's my *lunch!*'"

Stopping an Epidemic

Food-detecting dogs were especially valuable recently, when foot-and-mouth disease spread through Europe and elsewhere. In Great Britain alone, hundreds of thousands of animals were slaughtered and burned to stop the highly contagious disease. If it spread through North America, the loss of animal life and food products would be staggering. Drastic measures were necessary. Imports of meat and unpasteurized cheeses were banned. International travelers walked through disinfectant shoe-baths, and were asked not to go near farms. If passengers arriving from infected countries hadn't finished their airline meals, the leftovers were destroyed, in case even those might be contaminated.

In spite of all this, some people still tried to smuggle in food that might carry foot-and-mouth. Daisy, a beagle working for the Canadian Food Inspection Agency, checks passengers and cargo at Toronto's international airport; one day she found three suitcases stuffed with 55 pounds (25 kg) of meat wrapped in some clothes. "It was like they cleaned out the butcher shop before they came to Canada," marveled Daisy's handler, Mike Smith.

A mountain of meat is an easy find for Daisy. Another day, though, she indicated luggage and Mike couldn't find any food at all. What was Daisy smelling? The passenger finally remembered that she'd had some cheese in her bag in England, but she'd thrown it away before she got on the plane. The mere fact that the cheese had been there was enough to tickle Daisy's nose.

Fishing for Trouble

Bob MacDonald works in British Columbia as a "fish cop" for Fisheries and Oceans, the government department that protects Canada's marine animals and the places where they live. Bob's partner is a five-year-old German shepherd named Dart – short for d'Artagnan, the famous Musketeer. Dart is a big dog with a massive head and chest, and a bark to match.

Dart has the same training as RCMP dogs, and sometimes he helps with regular police work like patrolling and tracking. But his specialty is sniffing out illegal catches of certain animals that live on the sea floor: abalone, clams, mussels, oysters, sea cucumbers, and geoducks (pronounced *gooey-ducks*). "Dart knows exactly what he's looking for," says Bob. "When he smells something else, like crab or lobster, I can see his demeanor change, but then he realizes that, no, the smell isn't *quite* right, and he moves on."

Abalone-fishing is banned along much of North America's west coast, because the local abalone is in serious danger of extinction. It's against the law to catch the endangered shellfish, or even possess it. But abalone is a pricy delicacy – it sells for about six times the price of steak – so some people still sneak out to raid the abalone beds.

Crabs, mussels, and other sea animals are a different story. It's legal to collect them, but there may be limits on how much you can take, or when, and you may need a sport-fishing license. If you're selling your catch, you need a commercial license, which can be very expensive. It's not surprising that cheaters try to get around the system.

Conservation isn't the only issue here; people's health is also at risk. Some seafood is contaminated with E. coli – dangerous bacteria that get into the sea from sewage. Similarly, plankton (tiny sea creatures) sometimes contain a toxin (poison) that accumulates in clams and mussels and other animals that eat the plankton. People who eat those clams and mussels, and the toxin concentrated in them, can become paralyzed and even die. The most famous of these toxins is called red tide, because at times the plankton makes the water look red.

To protect both the sea creatures and the people who eat them, Bob and Dart keep an eye on beaches and fishing spots, and check out suspicious boats and trucks. When Dart finds something, he does what Bob calls the Hoover response. "Up comes his head, and he sucks up this long, huge intake of air – like a Hoover vacuum cleaner – and he barks once to be sure I'm paying attention, and then he does the big sit. I love the look on people's faces when I tell them the dog is trained to do this. When he hits on a load, it's a great feeling."

Many offenders didn't mean to do wrong. They didn't understand the signs warning about polluted water, or didn't know their catch was illegal; they were just collecting the family dinner. Bob confiscates the catch and explains why, and lets

🐾 *Bob and Dart check cars lined up for a ferry, in case anyone's taking home a contraband dinner. As Dart trots briskly down the row of cars, it's hard to believe he's working. But if somebody has a bag of clams, a cooler of frozen mussels, or even some dried abalone, he'll find it.*

them go. But there are poachers who make a business of breaking the law. Some are career criminals with long records of violent crime. They make big money out of selling illegal seafood to ignorant or dishonest stores and restaurants. If they're caught, the punishment is usually less than what they'd get for dealing drugs. If the abalone population is wiped out, or if someone dies of E. coli or paralytic poisoning – well, the poachers have made their money. And the risk is real. Beaches are officially closed when the E. coli count reaches 250 parts per million (ppm). Dart once sniffed out two hundred pounds (about 100 kg) of contaminated clams being sold to a restaurant, with an E. coli level of 3,500 ppm – *fourteen times* the legal maximum.

How does Dart feel about his work? "He loves it," says Bob. "I put a special 'find fish' collar on him when we look for seafood, and as soon as it goes on he just explodes. If we don't get right to work, he'll get impatient and nip me – 'Come on, come on, let's go!' His search drive is so high that I really have to keep my eye on him. Once, we were working our way through the bushes up a steep slope, and I lost sight of him. Neither one of us realized that the hill ended in a sheer cliff. Dart raced up the hill so hard that he went flying right off the cliff. It scared me to death when I looked down and saw him – the ground below was covered with sharp rocks and broken oyster shells – but he'd landed right in the middle of the only patch of sand. I rushed him to the vet, but all he had was a sore hip and a split lip."

Because seafood is so valuable, conservation is a constant battle of wits. Sometimes two poachers moor a small boat over an abalone bed; one scuba dives to collect the shellfish while the other keeps watch and pretends to be fishing. The stolen abalone is dumped in bags and towed to shore behind the boat. But if Fisheries officers stop the boat, the poachers just cut the line and let the bags sink. That makes them useless as evidence, because it's impossible to prove they came from the boat. So officers take a different approach: they wait till the criminals reach shore and hide their haul in a car. When Dart checks the car and indicates, Bob can search the vehicle, arrest the poachers, and confiscate their car, boat, scuba gear – everything but the clothes on their backs.

Professional poachers sometimes collect clams on a polluted beach at low tide, sneak them onto a boat, go out to sea to get legal clams, and mix the two lots of clams together. Dart foils them by boarding the boat before it reaches the legal clam beds, and sniffing out the hidden catch. Even if the boat stinks from years of fishing, his nose isn't fooled; he knows a clam from a clam-bucket.

Before Dart joined the department, it was hard to catch clamdiggers who went out on the beaches at night, because they scattered into the darkness at the first sign of the law. Now, Dart and some of the officers slip through the shallow water and place themselves in the poachers' escape route. When the poachers turn to run, Dart is waiting for them. Bob shouts a warning three times: "Stop or I'll send the dog!" If the poachers are foolish enough to keep running, Dart goes after them and captures them. "He's perfect for night work because he's almost all black," says Bob. "He doesn't show up at all. And even though he's excited, he always keeps quiet until I call the warning." When the dog finally does speak up, his size and his bark make him pretty scary.

But Dart has his goofy side too. "I remember one day he alerted on a truck. I asked the owner to open up the back, and all I could see was flats and flats of tomatoes. But I knew Dart must be on to something, so I told him, 'Find fish,' and he hurled himself into the tomatoes and started digging. What a mess! Chunks of tomato were flying everywhere. And then I heard him grunt, and he dragged out this immense sack of clams. He was dripping with juice, and he had a big gob of tomato on his nose, and he was just grinning all over."

People-Finders

Clams and mangoes aside, finding people is still one of the biggest jobs that dogs do for us. They help police put criminals in jail, and they help prison officials catch up with convicts who break out of jail. At border crossings, they detect people concealed in cars and trucks, trying to enter the country without the right papers. Between crossing-points, they patrol some borders with their handlers, looking for anyone sneaking across, tracking down people who have already crossed, and protecting their human partners on the job. Even more important, they search for innocent people: those who are lost, kidnapped, trapped, or wounded, and desperately in need of rescue.

When it comes to tracking people, it's hard to beat a bloodhound. Although some people imagine bloodhounds to be vicious and bloodthirsty, they are gentle

🐾 *Bloodhounds are often mocked for their sad-sack faces and their slobbery mouths. According to some defenders, the long, limp ears sweep up the scent, the baggy face traps the smell around the nose, and the goopy saliva helps the dog smell dried-up bits of scent. Whatever the mechanism, the dog's tracking ability is phenomenal.*

and affectionate – their name probably refers to them being pure-blooded. These drooling, droop-faced ground-scenters have an amazing ability to recognize specific people by their smell, and to track them when the trail is too old for most other dogs. And once they're on a trail, they're totally focused; they've been known to walk straight into a parked car, because they were so engrossed in the quarry's scent that they didn't notice the obstacle.

In one case, a burglar broke into a business by prying a rock up out of the mud and using it to smash a window. A police bloodhound named Cleopatra got the thief's scent from three finger-holes the man had left in the mud. The burglar was soon caught, and the loot was recovered. To honor the memory of Cleo, who made three hundred successful searches during her career, the National Police Bloodhound Association gives an annual Cleopatra award to the year's top police or search-and-rescue bloodhound.

Search-and-Rescue (SAR) Dogs

Some SAR dogs are professionals employed by rescue services, but many are volunteers. They are family pets who train and practice regularly with their owners so they can be called out to find people who are lost or injured in the wilderness, or trapped by disasters such as floods, hurricanes, and earthquakes. This work takes more than a good nose; SAR dogs need tremendous agility, endurance, self-confidence, and persistence. They have to work amid rubble, climbing over, under, and around, checking any space that might possibly hold a victim. "They're crawling on their bellies and squeezing through things," says one SAR handler. "It's incredible to watch." And they have to do all this, and concentrate on their job, in the midst of horror and chaos.

Some SAR dogs – especially Newfoundlands – specialize in water rescue. They can swim out and drag people to safety, or carry a line to or from an endangered boat so that rescuers on land can haul the boat in. A very strong dog may even tow a small boat to shore.

Gracie, a Norwegian elkhound – an energetic spitz with a dark, dense coat – had just started search-and-rescue training when a massive flood hit the Ohio River Valley, and Gracie and her owner, Ed Jagodzinski, were called out to help. They arrived at the scene to find houses knocked over or swept away, sidewalks torn up, cars heaped in piles, and everything mired in deep mud. All the buildings and ruins had to be searched for victims. Firefighters checked each building for safety, and then the dog teams moved in, working their way through every hole and corner. As the smallest dog on the job, Gracie was lifted into tight spots where other dogs wouldn't fit. She and Ed worked for a day and a half, finding one dead human and many dead animals – and one live cat who was safely rescued.

In recent years, SAR dogs have become renowned for their grim, patient work at finding victims in the wreckage from terrorist acts, such as those at the Oklahoma City federal building, New York's World Trade Center, and the Pentagon. Sometimes they lead rescuers to survivors trapped in the rubble; too often, what they find is a body. This is essential work, saving human rescuers many hours of desperate and dangerous searching, but it's stressful for the dogs as well as the handlers.

🐾 *An urban SAR team searches the wreckage of the World Trade Center. If the dogs work all day and never find anyone alive, they may feel guilty, as if it's their fault. Often the handlers finish the shift with a make-believe hunt that turns up a live "victim," so the dogs' day, at least, ends on a happy note.*

Dogs who train for search-and-rescue work may become specialists in a certain field. Cadaver dogs search for bodies at disaster scenes, but they are also called out when police suspect that a missing person has died. Forensic dogs also specialize in finding cadavers, but they are used more for finding long-dead bodies, especially those that have been hidden or buried.

One dog in Michigan has moved from detective to archeologist. Part Doberman pinscher and part German pointer, Eagle started his career finding lost people and bodies, but now he and his own owner, Sande Anderson, track down ancient human remains. When some bones were found in a field where a developer was building a subdivision, Eagle traced the limits of a long-lost 1800s cemetery by picking out fifty-five old gravesites. When historians were trying to map a battlefield from the War of 1812, Eagle pointed the way by sniffing out scraps of soldiers' remains.

Normally, it takes years of research and excavation to confirm the exact sites of old battles; Eagle did the job in a few hours.

Some dogs can even find cadavers under water. When someone drowns – or when a murder victim is dumped in a river – the body may be swept away by the current. If the water is murky, it's difficult for divers to search a large area. That's when a water-search dog may be called in.

These dogs can't smell the actual corpse through the water, but they learn to recognize the gases that escape the decomposing body and rise to the surface. The dogs either travel along shore or ride in a small boat, and they alert when a patch of water smells suspicious. Divers then search the area until they recover the body.

Buried Alive

On a clear day, a snowy mountainside suggests nature at its most serene. But snow masses are complex and dangerous. They are immensely heavy, yet unstable and inconsistent. At the slightest disturbance – or no disturbance at all – thousands of

A Very Close Call

Over three hundred dog teams worked at the ruins of the World Trade Center. One dog almost died there. Servus, a Belgian Malinois, skidded face-first down a deep slope of dirt and rubble. He was injured, and his breathing passages and lungs were so packed with concrete dust that he could hardly breathe. Servus's handler, police officer Chris Christensen, managed to extricate his dog, and he shouted for help. While he tried to clear the dirt out of the dog's nose, other rescuers applied first aid and put Servus on an intravenous drip. By now, the dog was having convulsions. He was loaded onto a stretcher, carried to a police car, and rushed to an animal hospital.

Servus recovered from his injuries, but Chris is still shaken. Servus has saved his life twice. "I can't believe I nearly lost him," he says. "I just couldn't let him die."

tons of snow can collapse down a hill in an avalanche. That's why popular ski regions mark approved hills where the snow is carefully monitored and controlled. Even so, some thirty to forty people die in North American avalanches every year.

Mike Henderson, a park warden in the Canadian Rockies, explains that when people run out of fresh snow on the approved hills, they may head into the back country. Too often, they don't have the skills they need to avoid being lost or stranded. They also don't have essential life-saving gear like a shovel, a probe (for feeling through the snow), and a transceiver (which sends and receives a radio signal). If they're buried by an avalanche, they're helpless and very hard to find. If they aren't found quickly, it'll be too late.

Here's the problem. While a few avalanche victims are killed by the force of the snow, or by the trees and rocks caught up in it, 93 percent are still alive under the snow after fifteen minutes. But as they lie trapped, their breath and body heat turn the snow around them into a thin shell of solid ice. They can't get out, and air can't get in. Unless someone finds them and digs them out immediately, they will almost certainly die.

That's where dogs save the day; in half an hour, an avalanche rescue dog can search an area that would keep a team of people busy all day.

Jeff Eckland was buried under an avalanche in California. At first he stayed calm, waiting for rescue, but then ice began forming around him, and he could hardly breathe. "The last three minutes, I was panting like a dog, trying to get air. . . . I started getting tunnel vision. The tunnel slowly started to close, and I was panting and panting and no air was coming. I thought I was history." At that moment, the ice shell was broken open by an avalanche rescue dog – a golden retriever named Doc – and fresh air flooded in.

Avalanche training is similar to search training, but the dogs have to learn the difference between the smell of a victim drifting up through the snow and the scent of other searchers. For practice, the quarry hides in a shallow snow cave with air holes poked through to let the scent out. Gradually the caves are made deeper, until the dog can find someone buried five feet (1.5 m) deep.

In some places, skiing outside the approved areas is illegal, and offenders are offered a choice: pay a heavy fine or be buried alive in an ice cave until a dog comes.

🐾 *St. Bernards are history's most famous SAR dogs. For centuries they rescued travelers lost in the snow of the Great St. Bernard Pass, in the mountains between Switzerland and Italy. The dogs were bred by monks living in the pass, and learned to follow the mountain trails through fog and snow. Weighing up to two hundred pounds (125 kg), they could haul heavy loads up the mountain, and their broad feet flattened the snow into a pathway. Despite the popular image, they never carried brandy kegs around their necks; alcohol makes a cold person even colder!*

🐾 *Anton Horvath and his dog Jason, on Whistler Mountain before a training exercise; someone is already hiding in a snow cave below. The team will go to a rescue any way they have to, from riding in a Snow Cat (a snow-going minibus with treads instead of tires) to skiing in with the dog on Anton's shoulders.*

This is better practice for the dogs, since they have to find a person they don't know. It also gives the errant skier something to think about. "You dig your own pit," recalls one offender who chose to be buried. "The feeling of being trapped starts to envelop you." He says that's the last time he'll go skiing where he's not supposed to.

For avalanche rescuers like Mike Henderson and Attila, his German shepherd, getting there can be half the fun. Sometimes Attila rides a ski chairlift, sitting at Mike's side; other times she perches in front of him on a snowmobile, her paws on the handlebars. For more remote searches, they go in by air, harnessed into slings dangling a hundred feet (30 m) below a helicopter. After the search is over, Mike sometimes skis out with Attila trotting inside the V of his skis. At least, that's the theory. "Once in a while we get our paths crossed," says Mike, "and we end up in a big pile of skis and poles and dog fur."

Anton Horvath, head of the Canadian Avalanche Rescue Dogs Association (CARDA), points out that avalanche rescue calls for caution and expert knowledge. When CARDA's volunteer SAR teams move into action, they start by surveying the area, checking topographical (land shape) maps, and digging test pits in the snow, to determine whether another avalanche is likely. They carry plenty of rescue equipment, and they always work in teams, taking turns going through danger spots, with someone watching from a safe place, ready to help or call for rescue if necessary. "Training the dogs is easy," says Anton. "Training the people takes years."

CHAPTER SIX

Dark Days – Dogs Go to War

Dogs are the best piece of equipment the Army ever invested in.
They're always on duty. You could trust your life with them.
– Steve Mac Robbie, retired army dog-handler

As spears, swords, and bows and arrows were replaced on the battlefield by guns large and small, dogs no longer went into battle as warriors. They were too easily shot, and they couldn't shoot back, and any armor heavy enough to protect them would slow them down and get in their way. But they were still called upon for plenty of wartime work. Some of it was like the jobs they had done for centuries; some of it was entirely new. Some of it reflected the deep bond between humans and canines; some of it was heartless exploitation of the dogs' loyalty and trust.

Napoleon detested dogs, but during his Egyptian military campaign in the late 1700s he had local dogs chained to the city walls of Alexandria, to serve as sentries and guards. In the same era, dogs carried messages for the army of the Prussian king Frederick the Great – who doted on his Italian greyhounds, and said he had never met a dog he didn't like. In the mid-1800s, dogs worked as messengers during the American Civil War, and guarded army camps and prisoners. At the end of that century, they worked as scouts for Theodore Roosevelt's troops in the Spanish-

American war. In the 1900s, through two world wars and the Korean and Vietnam wars and countless other military actions, dogs and handlers worked together night and day, sharing terrible risks and saving each other's lives again and again.

Many handlers say they became closer to their dogs than they have ever been to a spouse, a parent or child, or any other human. Dog and handler learned to read each other's smallest signals. A perked ear or stiffened neck on the dog, a flick of a hand or a faint hiss from the handler, could mean that death was lying in wait around the next corner.

Halt! Who Goes There?

In addition to their amazing sense of smell and their good night vision, dogs have much better hearing than we have. They can pick up very high-pitched sounds – frequencies of about twice as many hertz (cycles per second) as we can hear. They also have an inner ear they can close off to block out distracting background noises. And if you watch a German shepherd listening to an unlocated sound – twitching one ear this way, scooping the other that way – you can imagine how efficiently those big, mobile ears must collect the sound waves.

Even as our technology improved, dogs continued to lend us their ears. At home, they guarded munitions factories, prison camps, airfields, and radar installations. They walked borders and coastlines, watching for spies and other enemy intruders. On board ship, they warned of approaching enemy planes. Overseas, they patrolled or stood watch at military bases with human sentries.

On the battlefield, if a dog was placed at each end of a defended position, the handlers could triangulate, intersecting the compass bearings from the direction each dog alerted to pinpoint the enemy's position and calculate how much closer the enemy had advanced. In bivouacs (makeshift camps), the dogs curled up beside the weary soldiers, one ear perked. It's been said that soldiers never sleep better than when they have a trusted pooch snoozing nearby.

Message Runners

Dogs have been sneaking secret messages past the enemy since the days of ancient Rome. As late as the First World War, communication was a major problem for the military. Field telephones often failed to work. Signal lights became useless in rain or fog or the smoke of war. Human messengers were gunned down as they scrambled over rough terrain. But a message could be sent by dog, and a dog made a small, fast-moving target racing over fields, leaping trenches and bomb craters, wriggling under barbed wire, fording or swimming rivers, loping unnoticed through towns. Sometimes the dog's leather collar had a special compartment for messages; sometimes the papers were rolled into a metal cylinder attached to the collar. The Russians, who had a huge K-9 contingent in the First World War, even trained "reverse messengers" to slip into enemy encampments and make off with any papers they could lay teeth on, such as maps and despatches.

Since the Second World War, dogs have had little work as military messengers. Most fighting is done from a distance now, and communications are carried by high-tech radio and satellite systems.

Pulling Their Weight

In war as in peace, dogs have pulled and carried loads for us. In the First World War, they dragged ammunition carts and machine guns, and learned to lie down, out of the way, while the guns were firing. They towed ambulance carts to the wounded, and dragged the wounded away. With guns firing and shrapnel flying, they made their way to troops pinned down in remote outposts, taking water, ammunition, and medical supplies.

When soldiers are hurt on the battlefield, they may instinctively crawl to a sheltered hiding-place. If they lose consciousness there, rescue parties may not find them. That's one reason why dogs have been specifically trained to go out – usually at night, after the shooting stops – to search for the wounded. They can learn to ignore victims who are already dead, and either rescue the survivors or lead medics to them. Large dogs have even been known to drag victims into a trench or crater, out of the line of fire, before going for help.

Newfoundlands and other large dogs laid telephone and telegraph cables so that commanders could communicate with their troops. With reels of cable fastened to their backs, they patiently walked the chosen route, while the cable spooled out

🐾 *In the First World War, many Red Cross "mercy dogs" learned to bring back a soldier's helmet or a scrap of uniform to show that someone was wounded and needed help. Other dogs had a short signal leash hanging from the collar; if a dog came back carrying the signal leash in his mouth, it meant he'd found a casualty. Notice the billows of poison gas behind this cheerful dog.*

behind them. Walking a predictable route, weighed down by the heavy reel, many of the dogs were shot by snipers.

The Nose Goes First

Even today, dogs are essential members of scouting and raiding parties. A scout dog and handler usually "walk point" ahead of the advancing troops – the most dangerous position. The dog can detect snipers or enemy soldiers waiting in ambush from a safe distance – as far away as a thousand yards (1,000 m) if the wind and weather are right. The dogs alert silently, so the ambushers don't know they've been spotted. (Bloodhounds were tried as scout dogs, but they weren't a success. They could smell the enemy, but nothing would make them keep quiet.) Dogs can tell which caves and fortifications have been abandoned and which ones conceal enemy soldiers. They can locate the enemy's hidden stores of ammunition and other supplies.

Dogs can learn to detect boobytraps, buried bombs, and landmines by smelling the explosives. Metal detectors find some mines, but they miss clay, ceramic, and plastic mines, and they're useless anyplace where there is too much other metal around. Also, dogs are better than metal detectors at finding deeply buried mines. They can even learn to spot fine tripwires laid across a pathway to set off a bomb if anyone tries to pass by. Perhaps they pick up the human scent on the tripwire; maybe they hear a faint vibration as the wire moves in the breeze.

A Friend in Need

Whenever dog-loving people are fighting a war, they try to take – or find – dogs to keep them company through the ordeal. A group pet – a mascot – is a symbol of the unit and its loyalty, but the pet is also a pal, and a reminder of life back home. After all, in wartime the majority of soldiers are young; many have never before been away from their families. At times they are lonely and frightened, perhaps sick or wounded as well. A dog is a friend in a strange and dangerous place; a watchful guardian through the long, dark night; a confidant who listens to their fears and miseries and never tells a soul. Perhaps one reason we take dogs into the darkness of war is this: we hope that, somehow, they will help us find our way back.

The First World War (1914–1918)

While some armies have been quick to understand how useful dogs can be in a war, others have doubted the worth of canine units. In the late 1800s, long before the First World War, the Germans were already building a force of war dogs. They had home-grown Dobermans, Rottweilers, and Weimaraners, and they bought Airedales and collies from elsewhere. Once the war started, as German troops swept through Belgium and France, they conscripted suitable dogs and sent them home to Germany for training as well.

At first, British authorities resisted using canines. Not until the middle of the war did they admit that dogs were needed, and then families were asked to donate their pets. An unlikely force was hastily made up of whatever breeds could be acquired, and the dogs were trained, exposed to the racket of gunfire and grenades so battlefield explosions wouldn't panic them, and sent to the trenches of Europe.

A few breeds were chosen for specific tasks. Since enemy messengers often traveled by bicycle, Irish wolfhounds – tall, leggy runners who can weigh a hundred pounds (45 kg) or more – were taught to chase them and knock them down. Keen-eyed greyhounds were ideal for keeping watch on enemy lines, barking an alarm if anything moved. Jack Russell terriers raced through the trenches and killed the rats

🐾 *Among the worst weapons of the First World War were poison gases such as mustard, chlorine, and phosgene gas, which burned the tissues of the lungs and caused death or permanent damage. This French team are dutifully wearing their gas masks — but how useful could the dog be, with his sensitive nose locked up in this contraption?*

that stole food and spread disease. Because automobiles were not yet reliable and gasoline was in short supply, large dogs pulled two-wheeled ambulance carts that had space for one man lying down or two men seated. In a campaign sponsored by the YMCA, small dogs delivered cartons of cigarettes to the soldiers in the front lines. All in all, about 75,000 dogs were involved in the war.

After the war, some of the dogs were lucky enough to go home again. One British private begged for permission to take his dog back, explaining that the dog had been wounded twice during the war and:

> I think he deserves to come home with me, as he has stuck to me through thick and thin, and when I was wounded and could not walk he stayed with me all through the attack under a heavy barrage for nearly three hours, so you can imagine how attached I am to him. . . .

But many dogs were destroyed at war's end, on the excuse that it would be impossible to retrain them for civilian life. Others were simply abandoned.

The United States didn't have a canine unit in the First World War; when the Americans needed dogs, they borrowed them. Yet one American dog did find his way to the muddy, bloody trenches of France.

While an army division was training in Connecticut, a homeless dog – perhaps a Boston terrier – adopted the men and shared their life. They named him Stubby for his little stump of a tail, and enjoyed his company and his antics. When the men were sent overseas, they smuggled their mascot onto the ship by pulling him through a porthole, and Stubby soon found himself in the midst of a war. He was astonishingly calm despite the endless noise and chaos. He even left the small safety of the trenches to hunt for wounded soldiers on the battlefield. The stories of his feats grew into legend:

He would warn the men of incoming mortar shells by barking or hurling himself to the ground, and once prevented the escape of a German spy by sinking his teeth into the seat of the man's pants and refusing to let go. Whiffs of mustard gas, too faint to be detected by the human nose, sent Stubby into a barking tirade that warned the soldiers to don protective gear. One time he roused a sleeping soldier just in time to get both his and the soldier's [gas] masks on. . . .

🐾 *Sergeant Stubby. Some French women heard about his courage and sewed him a fancy little blanket-coat; it made a handy place to hang all his medals.*

Stubby curled up with wounded soldiers, giving them warmth and solace. When he himself was hurt and taken for medical help, he made the rounds of the clinic and commiserated with the human patients. By the end of the war, Stubby was a national hero. He met three U.S. presidents, was promoted to honorary sergeant, received a gold medal from General Pershing, became an honorary member of the Red Cross and the American Legion, and led innumerable regimental parades.

Second World War (1939–1945)

In the 1930s, as the world edged toward another war, Germany again built up a force of war dogs. So did Japan. Once more, the United States and Britain were unprepared. At the end of 1941, when the Japanese attacked Pearl Harbor and America entered the war, the only U.S. military dogs were some sled dogs from the Arctic and a handful of sentry dogs.

By 1942 the U.S. War Department recognized the need for canine units, and an organization called Dogs for Defense urged patriotic citizens to donate Spot and Rover to the fight for freedom. Recruiting posters requested large dogs such as "Collies, Standard Poodles, Eskimos, Siberian Huskies, St. Bernards" and others, and over ten thousand dogs were trained to work with various forces. Each dog was tattooed on the ear with an official number.

Some of the army sled dogs were trained for search and rescue. When an aircraft was missing or downed, dogs and handlers would fly to the area and parachute in, and track down the lost plane. They could rescue the crew or recover bodies, and perhaps bring back valuable or top-secret items from the wreckage.

🐾 *U.S. Marine Benton Goldbatt and Peppy in Guam. Peppy was recovering from a bullet wound in the head. When the Doberman Pinscher Club of America offered to provide as many dogs as the Marine Corps needed, Dobermans became the Marines' standard Second World War dog. The U.S. Army preferred German shepherds.*

More than seven hundred dogs served with the U.S. Marines. Some of them were sent to help retake the Pacific island of Guam, which the Japanese had seized after Pearl Harbor. Before departure, the dogs were rigorously schooled. In addition to basic obedience, they learned to leap through stacks of open-ended barrels, scale wooden walls taller than a man, scamper along narrow poles (good practice for running across a log spanning a river), and leap over pools of water. They wriggled through fields while explosives went off around them and guns were fired overhead. The trainers even built a model of a ship's side and hung it with cargo netting so the dogs could get used to being hoisted in a harness and hauled on or off ship. Most of all, the dogs learned to be constantly alert for anything that looked or smelled or sounded suspicious.

Over the course of the war, the dogs of the Marine Corps served bravely, saving countless lives. Many of them died in the process, and some were put down (killed) after the war ended in 1945. But 559 dogs were sent back to the Marine War Dog

School in the United States. Some had to be destroyed because of serious physical problems, and a few because they had been so deeply affected by the war that they could never again be trusted in a family. The great majority – 540 of the 559 – were patiently retrained as pets, and went home with their original owners, their wartime handlers, or adopting families. If the retraining was an effort, these dogs surely deserved it. After all, the motto of the Marine Corps is *Semper Fidelis* – "Always faithful" – and who could be more faithful than a dog?

Dogs also worked with the U.S. Coast Guard. In addition to its usual rescue and ship-patrol duties, the Coast Guard kept an eye on the beaches, watching for enemy ships, spies or saboteurs trying to slip into the country, or spies on land sending messages to ships lurking offshore. Several thousand dogs worked in the beach patrol. A dog and handler would walk a section of beach, usually at night, clambering over slippery rocks, hunks of driftwood, and all the gunk and debris that washes up on beaches. Some of the dogs wore canvas boots to protect their feet from sharp coral and seashells. Worse yet were the alligators and venomous snakes that infested some of the shorelines.

Although submarines didn't officially have room for dogs, sailors often smuggled a small mascot aboard. In the tedium and stress of underwater travel, and especially "silent running" – when the submarine was near enemy ships and nobody was allowed to make noise – a cheerful dog was a welcome relief. Bored sailors filled the long hours teaching the dogs tricks, and making them identity cards, uniform jackets, and collars studded with service medals. These dogs were a far cry from the taut, disciplined scouts and sentries of other services, but they played an important role all the same.

In the Second World War, the most famous American canine was Chips, a mixed-breed who traveled with General Patton's army, guarding tanks as Allied troops fought their way through Africa and Europe. In Sicily, when four enemy soldiers began firing a machine gun, Chips leapt into their concrete pillbox (fort) and took them prisoner. Later that day, Chips and his handler captured another ten enemy soldiers. Chips was awarded a Silver Star for his feats, and a Purple Heart as well, since he was wounded during his heroics. He survived his injuries and went back home to his family when the war ended in 1945.

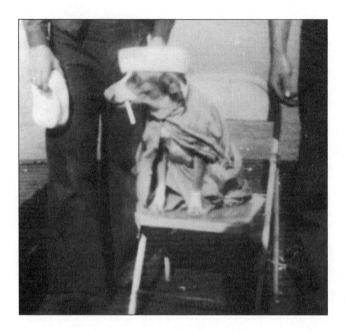

🐾 *Garbo joined the crew of the U.S.S. Gar when she was just a puppy. While the submarine was on patrol, she toured the vessel regularly and kept a fond eye on the crew. By making them laugh, she reduced the tension on long, nerve-racking patrols. "She should have gotten a medal for keeping our spirits and morale up when we needed it most," said one sailor. On shore leave, though, she sometimes had a little too much beer. At war's end, Garbo found a home with one of her shipmates.*

Unfortunately, some Americans thought it was insulting that a dog could be honored with a medal meant for people. Chips' medals were taken away, and it was decreed that American war dogs were no longer companions in arms; they were just pieces of equipment owned by the federal government, to be used as necessary and destroyed – not retired – when they could no longer work.

British war dogs didn't need people-medals; their courage was rewarded by the Dickin Medal, a bronze medallion given to animals who showed "conspicuous gallantry and devotion to duty" in their war service. There was Judy, an English pointer in the Royal Navy; Judy's gunboat was torpedoed, and she survived two years in a Japanese prisoner-of-war camp, barely escaping death from the prison guards. There was Beauty, a wire-haired terrier who worked for a pet-rescue squad in London, and found a total of sixty-three animals trapped in the ruins of bombed buildings. There was Rob, a border collie who served in the Special Air Services (SAS), and parachuted into Italy and North Africa over twenty times.

Another winner, Gander, has a sadder story. He was a Newfoundland who served with the Royal Rifles of Canada in their doomed effort to fight off the

❧ *Spike, an English bulldog, was just a puppy when he went to war with the U.S. air photographer Bill Morley. Spike put in three hundred hours of flying time with Bill, wearing earphones and a jacket with suitable insignia. But one day when Spike wasn't on the plane, Bill was killed. Spike was sent home to Bill's parents, but he was inconsolable and almost starved himself to death. In desperation, the family sent Spike to work as a gate dog at a Marines naval air station. Happy to be back on duty, Spike was soon promoted to sergeant-major for his "good record and morale building."*

Japanese attack on Hong Kong, and he defended his comrades numerous times. One day, an enemy grenade landed near some wounded soldiers. Gander had seen grenades explode before; he must have known how dangerous they were. He snatched it up and carried it away from his friends, and died when it blew up.

Vietnam and Korea

After the Second World War ended in 1945, the U.S. military lost interest in dogs, and few new dogs were trained. Then came the Korean War, in 1950. This war depended largely on guerrilla tactics, with camouflaged soldiers silently sneaking up on each other. Scout and sentry dogs were lifesavers, because they could detect ambushes and intruders much sooner than the soldiers could. K-9 units were hastily rebuilt, and it's estimated that, wherever they went, they lowered the rate of human casualties by 65 percent.

As the nuclear rivalry of the Cold War dominated the 1950s and 1960s, and war with the Soviet Union often seemed inevitable, dogs guarded airfields and missile installations against spies and sabotage. Meanwhile, a new guerrilla war was being

The Things We Do to Dogs

When dogs go to war, they suffer the same miseries as human soldiers: cold, fear, and hunger; disease, parasites, and injuries; physical and mental anguish they never forget. Beyond that, though, dogs have been victims of horrible schemes carried out in the name of war. They have been deliberately sent out to be shot, to show where enemy guns are positioned. They have been shot by their own army, to test new ammunition. They have been trained to look for their food inside or underneath armored cars and tanks, and then loaded with explosives and sent to blow up enemy vehicles.

Some cruelty is not so much vicious as callous and unjust. Despite the success in "deprogramming" war dogs and sending them home to well-deserved retirement, the view of dogs as mere equipment prevailed for years. Many dogs who served in the Second World War were left in Europe, to fend for themselves. At the end of the Vietnam War, virtually all the surviving dogs were ordered killed or abandoned. The handlers were devastated. Now, almost thirty years later, these veteran troopers still weep as they remember the way their partners were betrayed.

fought in Vietnam. Some four thousand dogs worked for the American side, doing their usual scout and sentry work, with some new twists.

The Viet Cong (the opposing guerrilla army) dug long networks of tunnel systems as a way to approach targets without being seen. The American dogs learned to search for the tunnels off-leash, following their partners' hand signals, and to alert by sitting just outside the tunnel entrance. The Viet Cong also dug punji pits – deep, camouflaged pits lined with sharp, filthy stakes; if the wounds didn't kill anyone who fell in, the infection from the filth probably would. But a scout dog could smell the pit, and would sit down in front of it and refuse to let anyone past.

For the war in Vietnam, the U.S. Navy built bases on top of floating platforms.

🐾 *American naval officer Roger Ortman and his dog, Arras, take part in a practice scenario, learning to combat high-threat terrorism.*

They were menaced by saboteurs who approached just under the surface of the water, breathing through straws or hoses and bringing explosives. Before long, dogs were circling the bases in patrol boats, sniffing out the intruders beneath the waves.

All in all, the canine units were so effective that the Viet Cong offered a cash prize to anyone who brought them the dog-handler's insignia from a uniform, or the tattooed ear of a dog.

Still Sniffing

Most recent American military operations – in Panama in 1989, in Haiti in 1994 – have included at least a few war dogs. In Operation Desert Storm, the campaign to liberate Kuwait from Iraqi occupation in the 1990s, eighty dogs worked as sentries, and sniffed out cluster bombs and plastic explosives; they all returned home safely.

Dogs are also helping us clear up the mess left from previous wars. Too often, hundreds of thousands of mines are scattered across roads and countryside during the fighting. After the peace treaties have been signed, the mines remain, and no one knows exactly where they are. Years later – decades later – innocent people are mangled or killed when they step on one.

❧ *Explosives dog Dick helps U.S. Army Staff Sergeant Richard Price investigate a bombing in Bosnia-Herzegovina that destroyed four new homes. The houses were being built as part of the peacetime reconstruction. Apparently somebody wasn't ready for peace.*

Anti-mine dogs aren't infallible – a dog may miss about five mines out of a hundred – but if two dog teams cooperate, each checking the other's work, their accuracy becomes outstanding. The United Nations has over two hundred mine-sniffing dogs in Afghanistan. In one year, they led mine-removal teams to about a hundred thousand mines.

After standing by us through so many years of combat and defense, war dogs are finally receiving more official recognition for all the help they have given us. Statues and other tributes are being erected. War memorial services sometimes take a minute to remember the canine veterans as well as the human ones. And in November 2000, American law was changed to say that after a life of service, military dogs can retire and enjoy the old age they deserve. They may be "equipment" while they work, but when their work is done, they can be part of a family once again.

CHAPTER SEVEN

Breaking Down the Barriers

Anyone who says these dogs don't understand what they are doing or believes that they are not doing real work has not watched the excitement it gives [my therapy dog] Sam and the undivided attention he gives to the clients he works with.

— Therapy-dog handler Betty Brown

For as long as dogs have been our friends, they have been comforting us when we are ill or in need. In the days of ancient Babylon, people thought that Gula, the goddess of healing, traveled with a dog as her assistant. Doctors in ancient Greece believed that a dog's tongue had special healing powers, and they let dogs lick their patients' wounds. Saint Roch, a Frenchman who was canonized for treating people who had the plague, was said to be licked back to health by his dog when he himself caught the sickness.

Sometimes, ancient cures prescribed for the patient had dire effects on the dog. In Cyanopolis (City of Dogs), in Greece, you could buy any number of canine remedies. For skin disease, there was a paste made from the blood and feces of dogs. If you were bitten by a dog and were afraid of getting rabies, a medicine or amulet made from certain parts of a dog was supposed to protect you. There were dog potions to cure baldness, and dog potions to remove unwanted hair. One way or another, a dog was good for what ailed you.

Even today, a number of people claim that a mole or sore their dog persistently licked, or even tried to bite off, turned out to be skin cancer. This may be more than folktale; experiments suggest that some dogs really can smell skin cancer. In the modern era, though, technology may win; chemical cancer detectors are probably more practical, and they don't need to go "walkies."

Second Sight

It seems that, for many centuries, blind people have followed their dogs on familiar routes. Illustrations from the Middle Ages show leashed dogs leading the way. In the 1700s a few organizations trained dogs for the job, but the teaching methods were crude and each dog learned only one or two routes.

Guide dogs as we know them didn't exist before the First World War. Many soldiers lost their sight in that war, because of eye injuries or poison gas, and they needed help to carry on with their lives. With so many canines serving in the war, trainers had a better understanding of how much a dog could do. A guide-dog school based on professional training methods was started in Germany, and gradually the idea spread around the world. Today there are guide-dog schools in many countries. One of them is Canadian Guide Dogs for the Blind (CGDB), near Ottawa.

Most CGDB puppies come from the school's own breeding program. Exceptional dogs, male and female, are chosen as parents and placed in closely supervised foster homes so that puppies can be bred as they're needed. Pups are sometimes traded with other schools so the dogs won't become inbred. (Dogs bred with close relatives are more likely to develop genetic flaws.)

Take Jobe, for example. This yellow Lab lived with his mother and her foster family until he was seven weeks old, and then he moved in with John and Heather Chilvers. The Chilvers were "puppy-walkers" – a nearby family who volunteer to raise pups. They got Jobe housebroken, taught him good manners, and took him to obedience class, where he learned simple commands: *down* and *no* and *forward* and – most important – *come*. If someone with little or no vision was going to rely on Jobe, he had to come every single time he was called.

🐾 *Image is a brood bitch; she bears puppies for CGDB guide-dog training. Image was first trained as a guide dog herself, but because of her calm, devoted disposition, she was chosen to be a mother instead. A brood bitch is like a queen among guide dogs; she's expected to produce healthy offspring, but, in return, she gets the best of everything.*

Jobe also had to be socialized. Heather says, "We take a pup to church with us, and to concerts, and to parades with horses and marching bands, and on trains and buses and planes. We get them accustomed to stores and offices and restaurants and playgrounds. We take them to farms and walk them past the animals. Guide dogs have to be comfortable in all kinds of places, with all kinds of people and animals."

Although the pups get lots of love and playtime, some games are ruled out. "We give them plenty of toys but no balls, because a dog who plays with balls might run after one on the street. And chasing squirrels – that's an absolute no-no. These dogs have to accept other animals as a normal part of life. How can you teach a dog that sometimes it's okay to chase a squirrel, and sometimes it's not?"

But how do you love a puppy and then give it up? Heather admits that it's not easy the first time, "because you can't help feeling that it's *your* puppy. But later you understand that you're just one part of a very special training process."

Jobe was evaluated throughout his training. Did he have the patience, confidence, intelligence, and willingness to do the job? Did he have the self-discipline to concentrate for as long as he had to? He had all of this. When he left the Chilvers, he spent about six months at the school, learning the guide-dog business from professional trainers. Then he spent another month there with the person he'd be guiding, while they practiced working as a team. Even after Jobe went off to his new home, the school stayed in touch to be sure the pair were getting along well.

Through breeding, birthing, puppy-walking, professional training, client training, and follow-up, producing a guide dog is a painstaking process. It's also expensive; it costs about $20,000 U.S. ($30,000 Canadian) to raise and train a dog. But the people who receive CGDB dogs pay just one dollar. All the rest of the money comes from donations.

Learning to See for Two

Let's follow Jessie, a chocolate Lab, through her training. She has to learn to lead someone indoors and out, in familiar surroundings and in places she's never been before. Although she must understand hand signals as well as spoken commands, she can't be too obedient. She has to have enough independence to disobey an order if it's dangerous.

Jessie learns to walk a straight line down the middle of the sidewalk, and to stop and sit at each street corner. (She can't judge stoplights; it's up to the person to listen to the passing traffic, and urge her forward when it stops.) She learns to turn right

---

Rule #46: No Dogs Allowed

Any member introducing a dog into the Society's premises shall be liable to a fine of one pound.

Any animal leading a blind person shall be deemed to be a cat.

(From the official rules of the Oxford Union Society, a debating club at Oxford University)

🐾 *Opal, a yellow Lab, keeps her rump at trainer Tim Morin's left knee. A dog guides from the person's left unless the person is unable to manage the harness on that side. Tim points out that, despite all the training, the dog is still a dog. "One day I was taking a dog through a supermarket — one he'd never been in before. I was curious to see where he'd head if I didn't give him any instructions. Off we went, down the aisles and around the corners, straight to the dogfood."*

on the command "Right" and a rightward wave of the hand. "Left" is more complicated; the command goes with a slap on the person's thigh, but if Jessie turns left she'll be pulling away from the person. She has to turn right instead, and walk a three-quarter circle so they end up going left.

Jessie learns that before she goes up a staircase, she has to stop with her front feet on the bottom step; before going down a staircase, she has to stop and sit so the person will understand the situation. She has to take one stair at a time, and hold herself back to match the person's speed. She has to recognize whenever something blocks the person's path, even if it's something she herself can fit under, like a ladder. If a sidewalk is partly blocked, she'll walk around the obstacle, but if she has to step off the curb to get by, she'll turn to face the street and stop and let the person decide what to do. If Jessie can't find a way by, she'll turn around and retrace her steps, and the person will have to figure out another route.

With so much on her mind, Jessie can't afford to be distracted. That's why it's so important not to pet a guide dog who's on duty. You can ask if it's all right to say hello to a dog who isn't working at the moment — one lying under a table in a

Follow That Cab!

Pets are often banned from places like stores and restaurants, for health and safety reasons. In the United States, service dogs are permitted to go wherever their work takes them, since people with disabilities are legally entitled to equal access. (In Canada the laws vary, depending on where you are.) But shop-owners or workers who are ignorant or inconsiderate – or who dislike dogs – may refuse to let these dogs in, even when the law says they must.

When the New York Police Department learned that some taxi drivers were refusing to pick up blind people with guide dogs, undercover officers went out with police dogs and pretended to be blind. It didn't work; their act just wasn't good enough. So the officers went to guide-dog school and learned to handle the dogs convincingly. Now, real guide dogs work part time as undercover police K-9s, helping officers crack down on cabbies who don't stop for the blind.

restaurant, for example. But the job has to come first, and confusing the dog – or the person – could be dangerous. So don't be offended if the person says no.

The most tempting distractions are other dogs. Jessie has to learn not to stop for doggy chats – maybe just a quick lick and a sniff if the dog is right in her path, but she must keep to her straight line. She also learns to ignore dogs who challenge her, backing down and "turning the other cheek" to their yaps and snarls.

Tim Morin has been training guide dogs for over ten years. Each day he sets out with a vanload of dog students and walks them through the city on a harness, one by one. At first they do short walks in quiet areas. Slowly the walks grow more challenging and last up to an hour. The pair go into stores and restaurants and buses. They tackle stairs and elevators, traffic and crowds, difficult corridors and doorways. Tim even tries to trick the dogs, urging them into the path of traffic, to make sure they refuse to budge until the way is clear. All the while, he is assessing their

Tim gives Opal some practice on an open staircase. Because the dog's eye level is lower than ours, the openings between the steps are much more disturbing — but she has to go up them anyway. They will also cross a narrow walkway with no sides except thin railings. But Opal is an experienced guide being retrained for a new partner, and she passes all these tests with flying colors.

comfort level, judging whether they have the skills and temperament for this demanding career. If the dogs don't work well enough, before or after graduation, they become pets in carefully chosen families.

Now that Judy Leung is through school and has a job, she and her young black Lab, Journey, lead a busy life. "My first guide dog didn't work out," says Judy. "She was fine in class, but in the street she was always going after food and other dogs. But Journey is great. It's much easier getting around with her; we take the subway together, and she's learned to understand 'find stairs' and 'find railing.' I find other people are more friendly and talkative when she's with me. She gives me companionship, too, since I'm living on my own, and she does really cute things. She's very playful for a guide dog. She gives everybody a kiss — anyone and everyone. She pulls me over to say hi to other dogs, and she's not supposed to. But we'll work all that out as she gets older."

Still, there can be awkward moments, when the dog makes a mistake or just decides to be mischievous. Judy has to remember to check Journey's mouth before they leave a shop like a dollar store, to be sure the dog hasn't picked some tempting item off a low shelf. Another woman remembers a morning when she felt that something wasn't quite right. All the way to work, she kept thinking she heard odd noises – giggles? snickers? When she reached her office, a friend whispered to her that her faithful guide dog had brought along a souvenir from home – a pair of her panties.

A woman who is a foster parent of guide-dog puppies recalls the day she took a young dog to the supermarket. "He was so well trained that I almost forgot he was with me, and instead of holding the harness I had it loosely on my arm. Without thinking, I reached into the meat counter with my left hand. He took it as a 'forward' signal and leapt into the display, right on top of the packaged meat! I scooped him out in an instant, and I don't think anyone saw. But I'll bet that little devil knew exactly what he was doing!"

All Ears

Since the 1970s, dogs have also been going to school to learn to help people who are almost or entirely deaf. Their lack of hearing puts a barrier between them and most other people, and it can make life frustrating and even dangerous. Imagine caring for a baby when you can't hear the child fall or cry. Imagine not being able to hear a smoke alarm or fire alarm, a burglar breaking a window, or an ambulance racing down the street.

Hearing dogs – also called hearing-ear or signal dogs – stay close to their owners, ears pricked for every noise. They learn to alert to many specific noises – the phone or doorbell; alarms of all kinds; the whistle of a boiling kettle, the ping of a microwave, or the sound of someone calling the person's name. They also alert to unusual sounds such as breaking glass. When they hear something significant, they paw or lick to get their partners' attention, and lead the way to the source of the noise.

This is one line of work where alertness, curiosity, and energy matter more than size. Terriers, miniature poodles, even Chihuahuas work as hearing dogs. But they need to be bright enough to learn many hand signals, and perhaps some American Sign Language (ASL). They also need confidence and initiative, because, unlike many service dogs, they don't wait for a command. It's up to them to take action, using their own judgment and experience to decide which sounds matter (a knock at the door) and which ones don't (a knock at the neighbor's door). One dog even tells his owner when the cat is scratching to come in.

Viva is a slim, dainty, sweet-natured black standard poodle. She works as a hearing dog for Cheryl Osten, and understands all the basic doggy words in ASL. When Cheryl babysits her young grandsons, Viva tells her if the children are fighting or making a racket. Several times Viva has used her body to block Cheryl's path so she couldn't cross the street when a car or motorcycle out of sight around a corner was racing toward them. "I feel much more comfortable when she's with me," says Cheryl.

After her early training, Viva almost failed the test to be a hearing dog. Petting is the reward she gets for doing her job, and the family was giving her lots of attention and affection without making her earn it. When they cut back on the praise,

🐾 *"Viva really understands the fact that I hear and my mom doesn't," says Cheryl's daughter Ruth. "Sometimes she comes to me first, if she thinks I'll get the message faster. And she'll do whatever's necessary to get Mom's attention — even jump up on her back, if she's facing away." In her spare time, Viva pays friendly visits to a nursing home for elderly deaf people.*

Viva got down to work and passed her test with flying colors. But she sometimes gets a little jealous of the other animals in Cheryl's house – two dogs and three cats who hardly lift a paw to earn *their* keep.

Hearing dogs take their duties very seriously. Although Viva is terrified of fireworks and thunderstorms, she always comes and tells Cheryl about them – and then runs away and hides. Another woman, Roxanne, found out how determined her dog Star was the first time she took Star to stay at her mother's.

> Star responded to the mother's alarm clock, rushing down the hall to wake [Mom] up. But Mom wasn't ready to get up and used the snooze alarm. Ten minutes later Star responded to the alarm again, and again Mom rolled over and went back to sleep. On the third ring, Star ran down the hall and bit the mother's nose.

Hearing dogs keep their partners safe on the rare occasions when there really is danger. Maybe just as important, they enable their partners to relax, day in and day out, in the knowledge that danger *isn't* sneaking up on them. The dogs also help their partners relate to hearing people. On top of that, they offer full-time company and friendship in a world that can be lonely and sometimes hostile.

Dogsbodies

Guide dogs and hearing dogs are both called *service dogs* (or *assistance dogs*); they serve and assist people who face barriers in life because of health problems. (*Therapy dogs* also work, but they give pleasure and comfort to people they don't know. Viva is a service dog for Cheryl, and a therapy dog for people in a nursing home.) But blind people and deaf people aren't the only ones who rely on service dogs. When Roberta Milstein learned that she had multiple sclerosis (MS), she couldn't think how she was going to cope. MS is a disease that damages the nerves, so the person gradually loses muscle control and may end up in a wheelchair.

Roberta saw a demonstration of how service dogs worked, and she was impressed by all the things they could do, but she wasn't sure about getting one. "I hadn't had a dog since childhood, and I didn't know if I could take care of an

🐾 *Thanks to Beardsley, Roberta can live independently, coming and going as she chooses. If she falls down and can't get up, she can send him to bring the phone so she can call for help. Beardsley also works as a therapy dog, visiting the children in a nearby hospital. Roberta explains the dog's work, and he shows off his skills and does a few tricks for the kids.*

animal." But finally she put her name on the waiting list. Two years later, Beardsley – a large golden retriever with a coat the color of caramel – came into her life.

Beardsley pushes doors open with his paws, and closes them by tugging on a rope or strap. If Roberta drops her keyring or wallet, he'll pick it up and give it back. He'll stand braced beside her so she can lean on his back for balance or push herself up using his support. He can even pull her wheelchair if necessary, perhaps up a steep hill, or through sand or mud.

Most of all, though, Beardsley is Roberta's friend. He senses her distress better than any human, and he'll stay at her side silently, patiently, for as long as she needs him. "Maybe you've had a dog," she says. "Maybe you know what dogs are like. But unless you have a problem like MS, you can't begin to imagine the wonderful things he does for me."

Most *special skills dogs* like Beardsley start life much the way guide dogs do. Puppies are either donated or bred for the purpose, trained first by foster families and next by professional trainers, and then – if they have the skills and temperament for the job – with the future owner.

Imagine that you're in a wheelchair and you want to wash some clothes. Your dog tugs opens the door of the laundry cupboard and hauls out the hamper, which has wheels and a pull-rope. You notice a dirty dishtowel hanging on a hook, so you get out your laser-pen and aim it at the towel; the dog fetches the towel, and you add it to the hamper. Then he pulls the hamper to the washing machine so you can put everything in. When the wash is done, he pulls the soggy items from inside the washer and passes them to you so you can decide which ones go in the dryer. Later, he'll fish things out of the dryer so you can fold them, and he'll pull the hamper of clean clothes to the bedroom.

A dog can get down the receiver of a pay phone, if it's too high for you to reach. Or pick items off a store shelf and pass money to the cashier. Or push a button in an elevator. A large dog can even help you go to bed at night. If you can get yourself sitting on the edge of the bed, the dog can squeeze in under and behind your legs, and boost them up onto the bed.

Special skills dogs help people with a variety of medical problems that make it hard to get around, such as muscular dystrophy, which robs muscles of their strength; rheumatoid arthritis, which makes joints stiff and painful to move; and cerebral palsy (CP), which makes the arms and legs stiff and hard to control.

Most of these conditions tend to develop when people are older, but cerebral palsy is something babies are born with. Thanks to their dogs, some children with CP can go off to school on their own with the other students. Pouches on the dog's vest keep books and notebooks within easy reach, and if a pencil or pen gets dropped, the dog is there to pick it up. Best of all, these children are no longer "that kid in the wheelchair." Now they're "that kid with the amazing dog." *Hey, is it okay if I pet your dog?*

More than twenty years ago, David Hawkins got hurt playing hockey and lost the use of his legs. Now, David is the owner/manager of a shop selling office products and services like faxing and photocopying. While he zips around the store in a

Who's Training Whom?

Where do you find people with enough spare time, energy, and love to train a service dog? Try a prison. In a partnership that's good for everyone, some convicted criminals are training unwanted dogs to help disabled people. The prisoners get doggy kisses for now, and career skills in training and grooming dogs to help them start fresh when they finish their sentence.

But why wait till people are in jail? In some places, troubled teenagers – who are at high risk of ending up in prison – are training service dogs. The dogs get the love and practice they need, and in teaching them the teens learn patience and self-discipline, controlling their anger and working past their frustration.

motorized wheelchair, he depends on his assistant, Jarvis, to turn on lights, pick up tools, open and close doors and drawers, and generally make himself useful. Jarvis is a golden retriever.

Jarvis is top dog when it comes to customer loyalty. "A few people see my wheelchair and they shy away, feeling uncomfortable," says David. "But when they see the dog beside me, they seem to warm up." In fact, people go out of their way for the pleasure of doing business with Jarvis.

Parkinson's

When people get Parkinson's disease, the nerve centers controlling their muscles gradually stop working properly. They may have trembling or rigid muscles; they may lean over or even fall down; their muscles may suddenly "freeze" and not work at all.

Service dogs are just starting to learn to help people with Parkinson's. The dogs have to be large; if the person leans to one side, the dog has to lean the other way, to balance things. "They're like a four-legged cane," says one trainer. If the person does fall down, the dog serves as a support in getting up again.

One of the first Parkinson's dogs, a black Labrador called Pax, has moved in with Ian Pearson. Ian used to be embarrassed to walk down the street, because people stared at his slow, jerky movements and thought he was drunk or mentally ill. Now they see the big, handsome dog in harness, and realize that Ian's fighting a physical disability. He can walk with confidence again. If his leg muscles freeze, he just says, "Touch foot," and Pax presses one paw over Ian's foot; this wakes up Ian's nerves, and he can move again.

Epilepsy

Epileptic seizures are caused by bursts of electrical activity in the brain. In a severe seizure, the person falls down unconscious and jerks violently on the floor, and recovers quite slowly. A seizure that happens in the wrong place – in a pool or bathtub, in traffic, on a staircase – can be very dangerous.

Wendy Baranowski developed epilepsy after having brain surgery. For a while she was having so many severe seizures that she had to give up her job and most of her activities. But now Wendy has a service dog, part poodle and part Labrador, named Ruby. When Ruby presses herself against Wendy, it means the dog has somehow sensed that a seizure is coming in about half an hour. The early warning gives Wendy time to lie down in a safe place where she won't get hurt. If Ruby won't let Wendy go up or down stairs, it means the seizure is about to start.

Knowing that a seizure won't catch her by surprise, Wendy has been able to get her life back. Not only that, but her epilepsy has improved. People have more seizures when they're tired and stressed. By helping them relax and live a more normal life, service dogs can actually cut down the number of seizures.

There are untrained dogs who sense when someone's about to have a seizure, and give their own warnings: they may whine or bark, paw or lick the person, block his path, nudge him toward a safer place, or go for help. One woman says that if she's in the bathtub when a seizure is approaching, her dog pulls out the plug!

These days, though, *seizure dogs* are trained to offer more than a warning. When the seizure is over, they may bring a blanket or a telephone. If the person is too weak to talk, the dog will bark for help. Some dogs even have an emergency phone button they can press to dial for help.

Diabetes

The sugar in our blood is the fuel our bodies run on. People with diabetes sometimes don't have enough sugar in their blood. If they're awake when this happens, they can quickly eat or drink something sugary. But if they're asleep at the time, their blood sugar drops lower and lower, and it's possible for them to slip into a coma and die.

Alan Harberd has diabetes, but he also has a blood-sugar alarm – his collie, Sam. Sam lets Alan know whenever his blood sugar is getting too low. If Alan is asleep when it happens, Sam wakes him up.

How can a dog alert to something as internal as low blood sugar or an oncoming epileptic seizure? How does the dog recognize the problem before the person does? Some dog-lovers are convinced that dogs have psychic powers. Although scientists don't have a definite answer, they've suggested a number of more down-to-earth theories. Maybe changes in body chemistry make the person smell slightly different. Maybe the upcoming emergency creates minor physical signs such as muscle tremors. Or maybe the event causes changes in the nervous system – which uses tiny electrical impulses to send messages through the body – and the dogs sense the changes.

Depression

After having three operations on his heart, Michael Lingenfelter was deeply depressed. Antidepressant drugs didn't seem to help. "I lost the will to live," he says. "I lost my job and just sat around the house and vegetated." He even considered suicide. Then Mike's doctors tried a non-drug remedy – a golden retriever named Dakota.

Dakota had his own reasons to be depressed. He'd been abandoned by his first owner, he'd suffered heartworms (parasites that can kill a dog), and he'd had surgery for a broken hip. But he appointed himself Mike's best friend, cheering him up, dragging him out for walks, and reviving his interest in life.

But that was only the start. Mike has bouts of very bad chest pain, and Dakota somehow senses an attack several minutes before Mike feels it. With advance warning, Mike can take his medication before the pain starts. Then he lies down and holds onto Dakota, slowing his breathing to the pace of the dog's, until the pain goes away.

Early one morning, in his fourth year on the job, Dakota sensed that something more serious was happening. He tried desperately to rouse Mike and his wife. Finally she woke up and called an ambulance, and Mike was rushed to hospital. He was having a heart attack. Thanks to Dakota, he survived.

Mike is back at work now, but he's not alone. Dakota goes with him, and helps everyone in the office feel a little more relaxed. At the end of the day, the pair visit hospitals and schools for disabled children, where Dakota puts in hours of overtime working as a therapy dog.

Narcolepsy

Joan Bennett has a sleep disorder called narcolepsy. With little or no warning, she loses conscious control of her muscles and can't speak. She may stay on her feet, or she may collapse and lie with her eyes closed, yet she can hear everything going on around her. After a few minutes she regains control, but she may still be very drowsy.

Joan's special skills dog is Morgan, a standard poodle the color of charcoal, with a great woolly pompom of hair on his head. At home he's curious and playful, but away from home he's a vigilant guardian. He won't let Joan cross a street until she says "Forward" – the fact that she can speak proves she's in control of her actions. "At first I sometimes forgot to say anything, and Morgan stopped dead and just about pulled me off my feet."

When a narcoleptic attack is beginning, there are subtle clues that Joan herself doesn't notice. She becomes quieter and moves more slowly, and tends to limp or weave as she walks. "The [dog-training] school videotaped me and identified these clues," she says, "and the dog trainers imitated them. That's how they taught Morgan to recognize an attack."

When he spots an attack coming on, Morgan finds Joan a safe place to sit or lie. If she loses muscle control, he guards her and keeps her safe while she's helpless. "That's why I have a big black dog," says Joan. "He stands over me and stares down anyone who tries to come close. People take a big black dog more seriously." After an attack, if Joan is in a safe place, Morgan will let her sleep for a while – but if

🐾 *When Joan goes out, she wears Morgan's leash attached to her belt. That way her hands are free, and there's no risk of her dropping the leash during an attack. "But I'm the one wearing the collar and leash," she says. "It took me a while to get used to that idea!" Her attacks are often triggered by strong emotion. It could be worse; in some people, narcolepsy is triggered by laughter. "They literally can't stand to laugh. Imagine living with that!"*

someone calls her name, he'll nudge her to wake her up. "I've had dogs all my life," says Joan, "but I've never had another dog like Morgan."

What Else?

Service dogs are learning to help with a host of other problems. For some disorders, the dog gives advance warning of an attack so the person can arrange to be safe. For others, the dog fetches medicine. Some dogs even open the refrigerator and get out a bottle of water, to help with pill-taking. For all these conditions, the dog offers the comfort and reassurance of a friend who's always there to help.

What conditions? There's fibromyalgia, which causes pain and disabling exhaustion. There's asthma, which makes breathing difficult; a severe asthma attack can be life-threatening. Like epileptic seizures, asthmatic attacks often appear when people are feeling stressed, so just having the dog around can help prevent an attack.

Dogs can even help people with psychiatric problems such as agoraphobia (fear of open spaces), panic attacks (sudden, overwhelming feelings of terror), posttraumatic stress disorder (disruption of present-day life because of terrible memories), and bipolar disorder (alternating deep depression and uncontrollable "highs").

Just Visiting

Some people aren't able to take care of a dog; maybe they can't even take care of themselves. That's why *visitation dogs* stop by places like hospitals, hospices, mental institutions, and shelters and soup kitchens. Visitation dogs are usually family pets whose owners work as volunteers. Often, both the dogs and the handlers have been tested and certified as therapy dogs – dogs who work at making people feel better, physically and emotionally. Together, the dog and handler go from room to room, offering each person a few minutes of company and friendship.

Imagine an elderly man sitting alone in a nursing home, lost in the confusion of Alzheimer's disease. (Alzheimer's is a form of dementia; people with dementia remember poorly and have trouble thinking things through.) He doesn't talk to the staff; he's not sure who they are, and he has nothing to say to them. He's isolated, unable to put his feelings into words. But when a dog comes in and lays her head on his knee and looks up at him, he feels a connection. He strokes her head, feels the softness of her ears. "You're a good dog," he tells her – the first time he's spoken all day. Perhaps he'll say a few words to the handler. Perhaps he'll remember that he once had a dog; perhaps the handler will get him talking about his dog. Even a brief visit with the dog can build a small bridge between this lonely man and the rest of the world.

Visitation dogs are especially helpful to small children who are sick, because they find it hard to communicate, and they often don't understand what's happening to them.

Blue is a big, placid golden retriever with a smooth white face and a thick, honey-blond coat. For the past seven years, Blue and his owner, Frank Miller, have been working as volunteers at Toronto's Sick Children's Hospital. They're teamed up with Katherine Packer and Bertie.

Bertie is a Shih Tzu. Like Blue, he's a certified St. John Ambulance therapy dog, with an official bandana and photo ID to prove it. Both Bertie and Blue are special-

🐾 *Left: Blue started life as a puppy in a guide-dog program, and went to live with Frank Miller as a foster pup. When it turned out that Blue had a hip problem and couldn't handle the job of a guide dog, Frank adopted him. Blue and Bertie make a curious team — Blue outweighs Bertie by about six to one — but they're both experts at cheering up sick children.*

🐾 *Right: Bertie is a bouncy-flouncy mop of long black-and-white hair with a darting pink tongue at one end. He has the advantage that he can be lifted up into a toddler's crib. Nobody's lifting Blue very far!*

ists; very few therapy dogs are qualified to work with children. But the two dogs have totally different styles.

While Blue paces calmly from one hospital room to another, his great tail swinging gently, Bertie scampers in circles and wags his whole backside. While Blue rests his head on a bed and soulfully accepts a biscuit, Bertie dives head-first into Katherine's bag, rooting for chunks of lettuce. For kids who want a laugh, Bertie's the clown to give them one. For those who feel too sick to laugh, Blue offers silent consolation.

Little Lucas has had major surgery, and he's still hooked up to monitoring machines and an intravenous bag. He's grave and quiet as the dogs arrive. His mother says he's having a bad day. But he strokes Blue's head, and Katherine persuades him to throw a plastic hot dog for Bertie to chase. Soon Lucas is cheering Bertie on – "Come on, come on!"

Aidan is a toddler sitting in his mom's lap, clutching her finger for security. Silent and shy, he reluctantly takes the plastic hot dog and lets it fall. Bertie hurls himself on it in a frenzy. Aidan smiles and whispers to his mom as he drops the toy again and again.

Michael is six, and he's recovering from a serious car crash. He lies almost flat in his small bed, quiet and withdrawn. With a boost from Frank, Blue gets up on the bed and lies beside the boy, stretching his head out for a rub and a biscuit. After a few minutes, Bertie takes Blue's place, perching on a pillow and begging for food. Michael starts talking about his school and his friends.

In a town in England, there's a guide dog named Bill. He and his pal Ben are Jack Russell terriers. While they were living as strays, some vicious person deliberately blinded Ben. When the pair were found by an animal lover, Bill tried desperately to protect his helpless buddy. The two little dogs were sent to a good home, and with Bill constantly at his side – tugging him this way, nudging him that way – Ben soon learned his way around.

Dogs on Staff

Not all therapy dogs are just visiting. Some are live-in companions – *facility dogs* – in places like nursing homes. Some people in these institutions have always had pets, ever since childhood; having a group pet in the building brings back happy memories, and makes it seem more like home. If they've retreated into themselves, avoiding company and conversation, a dog gets them talking again, praising and admiring the animal, and remembering their own beloved dogs.

The dog helps their physical health as well. Petting a dog makes people feel less anxious and more relaxed, and that can actually slow down their heartbeat and lower their blood pressure, putting less strain on the heart and blood vessels.

Members of the Team

Therapy dogs also work as assistants to doctors and therapists. Jofi, Sigmund Freud's chow, may have been the first dog to play this role, when the famous psychiatrist was treating patients in the early 1900s. Jofi would lie calmly watching people as they unfolded their deepest secrets, and they seemed to talk more easily in her presence. Freud claimed that Jofi also helped him judge a patient's state of mind: she would move away from someone who was tense and anxious, but she would come within arm's reach of someone who was sad and depressed.

Some dogs play a more active role in the treatment plan. Suppose you've had brain damage, and you can't speak properly; you can practice talking by giving the dog commands. If you sound a little strange, the dog won't mind. Or suppose you're redeveloping your muscle strength and coordination after an accident or a stroke. You can brush the dog, walk the dog, play ball with the dog. (Throwing the ball to the therapist wouldn't be nearly as amusing.) If surgery or burns have left you scarred, the dog won't stare.

Dogs can even help therapists treat autism. People with severe autism have trouble connecting to others, and tend to live inside the walls of their own mind. But if they talk *to* the dog, they may be persuaded to talk to someone *about* the dog, and that makes a tiny chink in the wall cutting them off from other people. Because some autistic children need constant supervision, therapy dogs may live with them as canine "babysitters."

When No Words Are Enough

Therapy dogs can even be part of a rescue team, in their own way. In the aftermath of the terrorist attacks on the World Trade Center and the Pentagon, dogs consoled emergency workers who were heartsick at the death and devastation. A few minutes petting a dog – perhaps hugging the dog – seemed to bring the world back to its senses. Arleen Ravanelli was there with her Siberian husky, Shylo. "I really believe the so-called tough guys – the police, firefighters, and National Guard – needed the dogs the most," she says. "They had no one else whose shoulders it's socially acceptable to cry on."

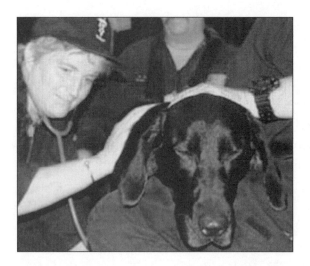

🐾 *Kinsay, a search-and-rescue dog with Texas Task Force One, hurt her paw while hunting for victims in the ruins of the World Trade Center. Even while she's being treated, she brings comfort to the disheartened crews. "If these dogs only knew what a difference they make," said one rescuer. "Certainly, there's nothing that can replace the precision of a dog's nose — and absolutely nothing that can replace a dog's heart."*

When relatives of the victims arrived to visit the disaster site, they were trapped in their private grief. Therapy dogs of all shapes and sizes were there to meet them. Dogs shared the boat ride to the disaster site. Dogs staffed the daycare, the counseling centers, the lineups for financial aid and death certificates. The families turned to the dogs for comfort, and before long they opened up to each other and shared their anguish. Dogs may even know, by smell, which people need them most, just as tracking dogs can distinguish "distressed person" scent; some handlers say their dogs headed straight for the people who were having the hardest time coping with the loss.

Many emergency authorities had been skeptical about how useful therapy dogs could be at a major disaster. What they saw in New York changed their minds. Father Keith Shuley, a Coast Guard chaplain who was also there, says, "I'm very experienced at this sort of thing. I can pick up on what people need pretty fast. But I can't pick up on it as fast as these dogs can." It's possible that in future, whenever search-and-rescue dogs are summoned to a disaster site, certified therapy dogs will be called in as well.

CHAPTER EIGHT

Top Dogs

Pal emerged from the water apparently totally exhausted, without even the stamina left to shake the water off of his fur. He staggered forward a few steps and then dropped down squarely in front of the camera with his dripping head between his paws and his eyes closed. The performance was so convincing and so filled with pathos that Pal got the role and began a dynasty.

— *Stanley Coren,* The Intelligence of Dogs

The year was 1943. Pal was a collie with a heavy white ruff, and a white blaze (stripe) down his forehead. He had just won the leading role in the first Lassie movie, *Lassie Come Home*.

Pal had already auditioned for the part, but he had been rejected – his head was too flat, said the casting experts, and his white blaze was too ugly, and how could a male dog play Lassie anyway? But Pal's acting and his fearlessness won him a job doing stunts in the film.

Then, one day, Pal got his lucky break. The star playing Lassie was supposed to jump into the surging waters of a flooded river and swim to the far side. She dug in her feet and refused to go. Pal plunged in and made the grueling swim in her place.

The director was astonished. He had expected to film the scene in five separate sections, but Pal had raced straight through the entire scene, from the dramatic start to the heart-rending finish. "Your dog is my star, I don't care what anyone says!" the director told Rudd Weatherwax, Pal's trainer.

🐾 *Pal, the dog who was called "too ugly" to be a star. Lassie was always played by a male dog — partly because males are larger and stronger, but also because females shed their coats twice a year (males shed only once), and all that shedding would have interfered with filming.*

Over the years, Pal starred in six Lassie movies. His understanding and adaptability amazed the people he worked with:

He never hesitated, never balked, always responded in the way that had been fashioned for him, and when something new arose, he handled it far better than most of the crew. He didn't even require stunt doubles as he hurdled walls, faked fights, pulled humans from swirling rapids, and spoke on cue.

Pal also starred in the pilot (trial) episode for the first "Lassie" TV series, in 1954. One of his sons, Lassie, Jr., then replaced him in the TV role. Eight generations of Pal's family have now played Lassie, in eleven movies and over twenty years of radio and television. Other descendants of Pal have worked as stand-ins for Lassie in certain scenes – especially messy ones, so the star could stay clean and fluffy.

Lassie became one of the biggest stars in Hollywood. He received thousands of fan letters, and answered them with "pawtographed" photos signed with an inky pawprint (made with a rubber stamp copied from Pal's foot). Lassie visited hospitals and wartime army bases, raising people's morale. He appeared at Red Cross fund-raising events. He endorsed Campbell's soup and Red Heart dogfood, his face smiling out from labels and advertisements. There were Lassie books, comic books, games, puzzles, coloring books – kids could even go trick-or-treating in a Lassie Hallowe'en costume.

Pal didn't just perform like a star – he lived like one. He had a bedroom to himself in the Weatherwax home. He had a luxury car (though he often traveled by limousine), a boat, and a private plane. He was welcome in the most exclusive hotels and restaurants. He even had his own small dog – what's a movie star without a pampered pet? When Pal finally died at the age of eighteen – very old for such a big dog – Rudd Weatherwax grieved for months. He could never again bring himself to watch one of his old friend's movies.

From Gaming Pit to Circus Ring

Pal may have been the most famous dog star of all time, but he certainly wasn't the first. Way back in the 1600s, when bloody amusements like dogfights and bear-baiting began going out of fashion, troupes of costumed, performing dogs became all the rage. They toured Europe, entertaining royalty and high society by dancing, playing cards and dominoes, and even acting out "dog dramas" on stage. In time, the dogs took their place in popular circuses.

These days, the expression "dog-and-pony show" means an elaborate event that's meant to impress people. (We might say, "Their party was quite a dog-and-pony show.") In the 1800s and early 1900s, dog-and-pony shows were small traveling circuses that couldn't afford more expensive attractions like wild animals. Larger circuses often included dog acts, too. There were races between chariots pulled by greyhounds, with monkeys acting as charioteers. (The monkeys apparently didn't enjoy this – they had to be belted into the chariots, and the reins were tied to their hands.) Greyhounds and Doberman pinschers leapt over obstacles as high as ten feet (3 m), taking off from a springboard (like a diving board) that was carefully hidden from audience view. Terriers climbed tall ladders, jumped into safety nets, and bowed to the admiring crowd. Teams of dogs waltzed and skipped rope and somersaulted on command.

🐾 *Dogs were important players in "The Greatest Show on Earth" as late as 1932. This was the time of the Great Depression, when many people could barely afford to feed themselves, let alone buy tickets to the circus. Perhaps the dogs were a temporary replacement for some of the more expensive wild animals.*

Some dogs just clowned around:

Clown dogs get to dress up like rabbits, elephants and little horses, and sometimes they can even have lights on their tails. They affect spectacles, dangly earrings, and pearl necklaces; learn to hold pipes in their mouths.... They tag along behind their comic bosses, with an occasional flipping somersault, sit-up, dead-doggie, hind-leg trot or front-leg balance. All that some dogs do is rush a clown and bite into his padded rear....

One Chihuahua learned to jump right through a clown named Polidor – or so it seemed. Polidor wore a big hollow "fat suit" with a narrow platform inside, around his middle. The dog jumped through a trapdoor in the clown's back, scurried around the platform, and popped out a trapdoor in the clown's belly.

Circus dogs worked hard, but they lived fairly well. Most of them were mongrels rather than purebreds, and many were homeless strays who had stumbled into circus life. At a time when spaying and neutering were less common, and litters of unwanted puppies were routinely drowned, they were lucky to find a family in the chaotic life of the circus.

From Circus Ring to Cinema

Dog-and-pony shows faded away as motion pictures became popular around the 1920s. Most silent movies had fairly obvious stories, since it was hard to manage complicated plots and subtle emotions without dialogue. Dogs made great silent actors, livening up the story and showing off their tricks – and it wasn't hard to guess what they were saying.

When filmmakers learned to add speech to movies, in the late 1920s, some famous stars became has-beens almost overnight; their profiles were stunning, but their voices were laughable. One star who easily made the leap to "talking pictures" was Rin Tin Tin. (In French, *rin-tin-tins* were lucky charms soldiers bought to keep themselves safe.) Rinty was a German shepherd born in Europe during the First World War – his father may have been a German ambulance dog – and brought home after the war by an American soldier. It's claimed that Rinty understood more than five hundred commands. He appeared in some thirty movies, and became such a huge star that he often got top billing – his name came first in credits and on posters, before the names of his human co-stars. There were years when he earned more money for Warner Brothers film studio than any two-legged star. Two of his descendants played Rin Tin Tin in a TV series. These days, some of Rin Tin Tin's descendants are working as real-life search-and-rescue dogs.

Dogs can serve a lot of purposes in a movie or TV show. They add humor and appeal – think of Beasley, the slobbering French mastiff in *Turner and Hooch*. They help the human characters seem like real people. Their cute tricks fill in moments when nothing much is happening – think of Moose, the Jack Russell terrier who plays Eddie on "Frasier." They give the actors a way to explain things to the audience

🐾 *This publicity shot is from an old Mack Sennett comedy, almost certainly a silent film. Animal acting falls into two categories: doing normal things (sitting, barking) on command, and doing things the animal would never normally do. How would you teach a dog, "Now hang your chin on this stool and balance a chicken on your head"?*

– think of Porthos, Captain Archer's beagle on "Star Trek: Enterprise," who hears private thoughts the starship captain would never tell his crew. And while dog stars require a lot of training and attention, they don't embarrass their employers by getting arrested for buying illegal drugs or beating up photographers.

Scott Taylor runs acting classes for dogs, and serves as an agent for his graduates, finding them work in TV, films, and advertising. For movie roles he deals with the wrangler, the person in charge of any animals in the film.

"When a movie calls for dogs," Scott explains, "the wrangler puts out a call to people like me. We're told the kind of dogs they want, and the skills the dogs need." Dog actors get their work pretty much the way humans do; sometimes the wrangler wants a specific star, but more often the dogs' portfolios are submitted. A portfolio contains the dog's resume – skills, acting experience, rave reviews – and a flattering variety of photographs. The best candidates are then called in to audition. Dogs or not, this is still showbiz.

But the strangest request Scott ever had wasn't for a movie. It was for man's best friend to be man's best man. Artyik, a pure white wolf/dog hybrid, was hired to wear a formal bow tie and attend a wedding in an ice cave – arriving by helicopter and standing up for the bridegroom as best man. (If you think that's easy, remember that the best man proposes the first toast to the bride and groom!)

Scott even got one dog, named Qualba, a job in cartoons. Qualba wore a suit, similar to a corset, that fitted her whole body tightly and had a lot of markers like ping-pong balls. As Qualba showed off her moves, she was filmed from all sides. A computer recorded her movements by tracking the ping-pong balls, and the same patterns were used for the cartoon dog in *Action Man* so the animation would seem realistic.

Behind the Scenes

How do people get into the animal-actor business? Anne Gordon started out as a zookeeper in Seattle, but she wanted closer contact with animals. When two orphaned lion cubs were sent to a wild-animal trainer in California – they had been raised by humans, and they couldn't join the zoo's lion pride – Anne went with them. She stayed in California to learn about animal training, working with everything from lions and tigers to chimpanzees and zebras.

Today Anne has her own business, training animal actors of all kinds, and she certainly has the close contact she was looking for. She lives with ten dogs, ten cats, two wolves, a deer, three raccoons, and a young beaver named Huckleberry who sleeps in the house and likes to help with the chores.

Although Anne trains her wild animals from infancy – otherwise they'd be too afraid of people, and she wouldn't be able to work with them – she gets most of her dogs from shelters. "Sometimes I need a certain type of dog," she says, "but often a dog's look just strikes me."

Anne's dogs learn fairly standard obedience skills, following hand signals as well as verbal commands, but they need stage training too. Speaking is very important; they have to bark on cue. Some dogs learn more than one bark – maybe a friendly *arf* and a threatening *rrrrowf.* They also learn to do clever things with their paws. Most important, they learn about marks.

Suppose an actor – human or canine – is supposed to run into a scene, and stop and speak. The camera operator has to know where the actor will stop, to focus the camera on that exact position. So a small mark is made on the floor. The actor stops on the mark, and the speech is filmed in sharp focus. Dogs have to stop right on their marks too, whether they are moving away from the trainer or coming toward her. "It can be more confusing than it sounds," Anne says. "I have to be in a place where I can send them off or call them back. But with the cameras swinging around to catch all the action, it's sometimes hard for me to stay out of sight. I may be hiding behind a tree, or around a corner. The dogs have to remember where to find me."

Fortunately, the dogs don't need as much cosmetic attention as their human co-stars. Usually Anne keeps them clean and brushed. For a dog with a fancier coat, like a poodle, a groomer is sometimes hired. When several dogs are sharing a role, there may be an animal colorist to make sure they look the same; although their spots and markings will be dyed to match, the hair grows out quickly, so the dogs often need

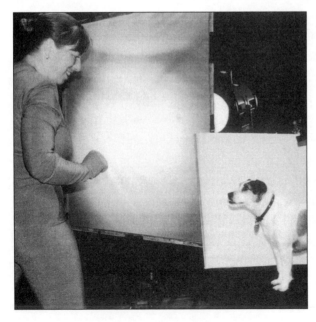

🐾 *For the Stephen King miniseries "Rose Red," Poppy – a Jack Russell terrier – played the role of Buddy, who bites a girl and is sent flying, head over heels, by her telekinetic powers. How could Poppy manage the acrobatics? She did a great leap in front of a green screen, which doesn't show up on film. While Poppy was in the air, the camera was rotated. When the footage was added to the film of the girl, it seemed that Poppy was being hurled away. Since Anne was in front of the camera too, she had to wear a lime-green bodysuit so she wouldn't show on the film. "I felt pretty conspicuous out there, with everybody else in normal clothes," she says.*

touchups. And when the dog's role involves being "injured," it's the colorist who paints on the gory wounds.

Rusty, Anne's border terrier, played Quark in the TV series "Honey, I Shrunk the Kids." Mingo, her terrier mix, appears at the beginning of the movie *Snow Day*; when the mean school principal is hit by a snowball and drops the steak he's barbecuing, Mingo snatches it and runs away. If Mingo caught a real steak he'd devour it on the spot, so that's a rubber steak he's making off with. (But he got a real one when the scene was finished.)

Work like this requires a dog's full attention, and scenes are often repeated again and again. The job can also be physically exhausting, if the dog is running or chasing someone. In the film *Air Bud – Golden Receiver*, the football-playing golden retriever is played mainly by Rush, who spent eight weeks learning all his maneuvers. But two other dogs helped with the running scenes, and another, Zak, lent his skills at sinking basketballs.

In *Turner and Hooch*, Beasley performs very dramatic stunts. In one scene he bursts right through a glass window. How did he learn to do that? First his trainer

🐾 *This well-dressed bulldog, photographed a hundred years ago, probably adorned a business calendar. Was she a reminder that customers can be very demanding?*

put a paper pane in the window so the dog could easily jump through it. Then the pane was made of cellophane, which was harder to tear. Then the cellophane was replaced with light plastic. When Beasley was comfortable hurling himself through the plastic, he was ready to do the stunt – through a windowpane of "breakaway" glass that wouldn't hurt him.

Next time you're watching a dog actor in a movie or on TV, try to imagine the scene from the trainer's point of view. How would you get a dog to do this? If the dog performs a series of actions, how many do you think were done in one sequence, without stopping the camera? (Watch for the telltale moment when the scene shifts.) Did the dog actually do what you're seeing, or was there some film or camera trickery? Do you think it's always the same dog? And where is the dog *looking?* That's probably where the trainer is, just off camera.

As special effects grow more sophisticated, dog stunts become more extreme; the dog can appear to do almost anything. But computer animation is becoming faster and cheaper, and more and more convincing. Will movie technology reach the point where creations like Scooby-Doo and Hagrid's Fluffy replace flesh-and-blood stars?

Bringing Home the Medals

Not all human stars work in the arts; some perform on the playing field. The canine world has its sports stars as well, and its competition and trophies.

In the sport called agility, dogs scramble through an obstacle course, racing to finish it correctly in the shortest time. They run or crawl through tunnels, cross swaying bridges and teeter-totters, leap through hoops and over hurdles, scoot up stairs and down slides, and weave in and out through rows of poles. Since the human partner directs the dog through the many steps of the course, lots of teamwork is required, and long hours of practice.

Schutzhund is an altogether sterner form of competition. It started in Germany about a hundred years ago, as a way to preserve the fine qualities of working dogs at a time when many of their jobs were disappearing. By assessing the talents of many dogs of various kinds, and cross-breeding them to improve their performance, breeders gradually developed the dog we now call the German shepherd.

Schutzhunds (the name is German for "protection dog") are still usually German shepherds or similar breeds, and the skills they learn are tracking, obedience (in heeling, jumping, retrieving, and so on), and protection (finding a "bad guy," defending the handler, making sure the villain doesn't escape). To most police dogs this is all in a day's work, but many civilian dogs also win prizes as champion schutzhunds.

Greyhounds and whippets still work as professional racing dogs, running on a track while gamblers place bets. The events are impressive to watch – these bone-thin dogs can run almost 40 miles per hour (65 kph) over a short distance. (Why can dogs run so fast? One reason is that their shoulders are attached to the rest of the skeleton by muscle – not by bone, like ours – so they can bend their bodies much farther than we can.) These racetrack stars are often valued only for

Weird Dog Jobs

The business of arts and entertainment has some odd corners, and some unlikely dog jobs, too. In England, a black Labrador named Oscar the Hypno-Dog works as a stage hypnotist's assistant. In New York, a Jack Russell terrier named Tillamook Cheddar is a successful artist; by scratching and biting color transfer paper, she creates abstract works that are sold through art galleries.

Several sleek, languid Weimaraners – first Man Ray, and then Fay Ray and her puppies – have posed for hundreds of portraits by American photographer William Wegman. Draped in exotic clothing and hats, arranged coiled in furniture or splayed across it, the dogs appear in art and fashion exhibits, in advertisements, on greeting cards. They illustrate books of Fay's Fairy Tales. They've even taught arithmetic on "Sesame Street." Wegman persuades them to adopt striking and sometimes mind-boggling positions. "As far as Fay was concerned," he says, "the more difficult the better. She was bored with the easy positions. She wanted to impress." No matter how undoglike the stance, the Weimaraners' intense, endearing dogness shines through.

🐾 *Turbo does his famous back catapult off John Misita, to capture a flying Frisbee. John and his four dogs — "K9s in Flight" — travel around performing agility shows. Where does a star like Turbo come from? He was a stray, rescued from the street.*

their speed, and get destroyed when their short careers are over, so many people disapprove of the business.

But not all dog-racing is professional. Some people who have traditional sighthounds – Afghans, borzois, Salukis, wolfhounds, and others, as well as whippets and greyhounds – take their dogs lure coursing. In this sport, a tempting scent lure is dragged over open countryside ahead of time, and the course is inspected for anything that might hurt the dogs. Then the dogs are released to follow the smell. Like their wild ancestors, they have the thrill of racing full tilt in pursuit of game (or at least its smell), but at the end of the day they go home with their human families.

Championship sheepdog and cattledog trials show off the extraordinary understanding of a good herding dog, and the way a single dog can control a hundred animals or more. Following the handler's whistled commands, a dog can drive a flock or herd around posts and through gates, or cut off a single beast from all the rest.

What other events do dogs compete in? They play Frisbee and Flyball. Big dogs like St. Bernards and Newfoundlands compete in water rescue, or in carting (pulling someone in a lightweight cart or wagon). Smaller dogs go carting with teddy bears as passengers. (Some hospital therapy dogs show up for work pulling a cartload of stuffed toys.) But there's an extreme canine sport, as well.

Dashing through the Snow

Back in 1925, there were fears of a diphtheria epidemic in Nome, Alaska. Diphtheria can kill people or leave them disabled, but fortunately there's a serum to prevent it. Working in relays, nineteen sled-dog teams made a desperate six-day run, through a savage blizzard, to get the life-saving serum to Nome. Their feat is commemorated by a statue to one of the lead dogs, named Balto, in New York's Central Park.

The serum run is also honored every March by the Iditarod Trail, a sled dog race from Anchorage to Nome that covers almost 1,200 miles (over 1,900 km), through cliffs and mountains and dense forest, over frozen rivers and ocean, and across barren tundra. Sled-dog racing is a growing sport, and there are many other races, but the Iditarod is the most challenging and the most famous.

🐾 *Sled dogs in Alaska, eagerly awaiting the start of the Iditarod. Some mushers keep racing even after the snow melts by mounting their sleds on inline wheels.*

Alaskan huskies and malamutes are the usual sled dogs. (Malamutes are larger huskies, used mainly for hauling freight.) Other large breeds have been tried: collies, Dalmatians, Irish setters. But while they can run quickly, these southern dogs don't have the endurance and cold resistance of the Arctic dogs, who can run as much as a hundred miles a day. Some breeders have crossbred huskies and wolves, but with little success; although the two animals look similar, the wolf mentality is wrong for racing, and so is the gait (pace). On top of that, wolf/dog hybrids are notoriously unpredictable, even dangerous.

Sled-dog racing is sometimes criticized as cruel to the dogs. One reason is that they run for hours, sometimes through daunting conditions. But these dogs have been bred for centuries to pull loads across the ice. They do it as joyfully as a retriever fetches tennis balls or a terrier chases squirrels. "When the dogs see you coming with their harnesses, the whole line goes nuts," says one dogsledder. "Shrieking with excitement, flipping backwards in the air . . . 'Me *first!* Me *first!* Take me *first!*'" In their passion for running, they keep racing even if their feet are cut by ice, even if balls of ice form between their toes. (Dogs sweat through their feet, and the sweat can freeze into iceballs, so racing dogs usually wear fleece booties.)

A more somber argument is that some dogs are injured in the race, and a few die, from accidents and from the overall physical strain. Responsible race organizers do their best to protect the dogs through high standards of care and safety. Any dog who wants to stop running is loaded onto the sled and dropped off to be cared for at the next checkpoint. All teams are required to take long rest breaks during the race. Veterinarians keep an eye on each dog's condition along the route of the Iditarod, and give a special award to the driver with the best-treated dog team.

Setting up a sled-dog team is a lot more complicated than you might think. The dogs have to run in a balanced team, according to their individual strengths and weaknesses. Their speed and length of gait have to be matched so that they can work together. They're harnessed in pairs on either side of a central towline, with the faster dogs toward the front, behind an experienced lead dog who sets the pace. Two strong "wheel dogs" run right in front of the sled, to steer it and swerve it away from dangers.

Since the sled driver – called a musher – doesn't have reins to direct the dogs, they follow *gee* and *haw* ("right" and "left") commands. The musher has to understand each dog and observe them all closely, watching their body language to recognize when Blackie is getting lazy, or when Snowball is hurting. No good musher punishes a dog for running poorly, or pushes the team to run beyond its capacity.

Although the musher has a footbrake, it barely slows down a team of racing huskies. It's not uncommon for inexperienced mushers to lose their sleds entirely, and be left behind in the snow as the dogs charge gleefully away.

Keeping and training a team of sled dogs is pretty much a full-time job, and a hugely expensive one. But there are places where amateurs can try the experience of dog-sledding – as a passenger for a few hours, or as a tourist on a trip of days or weeks. In an era of snowmobiles and helicopters, there's still a place for the irrepressible, indomitable sled dog.

Putting on the Dog

With so many dogs working so hard to come first, it seems odd that some dogs win championships by the length of their noses or the tilt of their tails. But then, the world of show dogs – a world known as the fancy – is full of contradictions.

A Chihuahua may weigh as little as two pounds (less than a kilogram); a St. Bernard may weigh a hundred times that much. A Mexican hairless has only a slight fuzz here and there on its body; if an Old English sheepdog went for a walk and left its coat behind, you might never notice that the dog was gone.

The fabulous variety of the canine world has been created, for the most part, by deliberate breeding. Whenever we thought of a doggy task, we tailored a dog to do it. In breeding dogs to work, we also bred them to be healthy, since a weak or disabled dog might have trouble doing the job.

Now that we have this wonderful range of breeds, it's protected by the system of purebreeding. Dogs are not recognized as purebreds unless there are documents to prove that their ancestors were purebred. Kennel clubs issue the documents, keep track of purebred canine family trees, and try to make sure no dogs of mixed parents are passed off as purebred.

🐾 *The first official dog show was held in England in 1859. In earlier years, dogs had been valued largely for the way they worked; as shows became more popular, their looks had to meet carefully defined standards. Contestants were pampered, groomed, and fluffed to perfection. Some owners — spurred by large prizes and stud fees (the price of breeding with a champion dog), or by vanity and envy — took desperate measures: coloring the dog's coat, blackening the dog's nose, paying for cosmetic surgery. There were even stories of jealous owners poisoning rival dogs.*

When a new kind of dog is created by crossbreeding – such as the whippet, bred from terriers and greyhounds – it isn't considered a breed until it "breeds true." For example, the puppies of whippet parents are clearly whippets; they're not a random jumble of terrier and greyhound characteristics. Even when the dogs breed true, there is likely to be hot debate about whether or not they should be accepted as purebred. These days, cockerpoos (bred from poodles and cocker spaniels since the 1960s) and labradoodles (bred from poodles and Labradors since the 1980s) are popular and trendy, but neither is recognized by the kennel clubs.

At dog shows, individual dogs are compared to the breed standard; if the shape isn't exactly right, if the coat has non-standard coloring, the dog is not acceptable for breeding. The rules are strict, but the goal is to make sure that in a hundred years or five hundred years, Chihuahuas and St. Bernards and all these other wonderful breeds will still be the dogs they are today.

Unfortunately – like the emperors of China – we have fussed too much about the way many breeds look. If a small dog is cute, then surely a smaller dog should be cuter? If a squinched-in face is adorable, surely the squinchier the better? As more and more dogs were pets rather than laborers, breeding standards – for big dogs as well as lapdogs – focused on appearance. Inherited problems of health and behavior were often ignored, and passed from one generation to the next. Inbreeding made the flaws worse; for example, if brother and sister dogs both suffered a slight defect, and they were mated, the defect might be much worse in their puppies.

As a result, certain breeds are now more likely to develop crippling bone and joint conditions. Some suffer ear or eye infections because, over the generations, their faces have been distorted. Some become blind or deaf. Some are plagued by allergies or digestive upsets or epilepsy. Some tend to be jittery and snappish; some display "sudden rage syndrome," turning savage with no warning.

Good breeders are doing their best to weed out the problems, examining all puppies carefully and making sure that only the healthiest are used for breeding. But purebred pups can be sold for a considerable price, and irresponsible breeders may ignore hereditary defects, knowing that they probably won't become obvious until the dog is older. In the worst breeding operations – known as puppy mills – parent dogs are kept in horrible conditions, while the breeders churn out as many pups as they can possibly sell.

Fortunately, change is in the wind. As we learn more about canine genetics and DNA, it's easier to find the defective genes that carry hereditary problems. As sports like agility training and lure coursing gain popularity, people are more insistent about getting a healthy, intelligent dog. Through more thoughtful breeding, we should be able to preserve dogs who not only look like their ancestors, but have their other wonderful qualities as well.

CHAPTER NINE

The Personal Pooch

> You didn't have to throw a stick in the water to get him to go in. Of course, he would bring back a stick if you did throw one in. He would even have brought back a piano if you had thrown one in.
>
> *— James Thurber*

The dogs who share our own lives — snoozing on the bed, drooling by the dining table, gnawing idly on a handy chair leg — may seem far removed from those well-regimented K-9s and those devoted service dogs. But make no mistake — a family dog is a working dog, too.

Guard dog? You bet. No matter how big or small the dog is, that alarm bark (or yip or woof) says, "Come one step closer to my home and family and I'LL DEAL WITH YOU!" Most of us sleep better with a dog on guard, and no wonder. A dog is such a good burglar deterrent that dogless people sometimes keep a very large dog dish by the door, to scare off prowlers. Many runners and joggers feel safer with a dog loping alongside. At least one hotel employs an escort dog who accompanies guests when they run.

Therapy dog? Dogs have a great sense of how we're feeling, and they do their best to respond when we're miserable. Like professional therapy dogs, they help us relax when we are tense, bringing down our pulse rate and blood pressure. We are more likely to be healthy and long-lived if we share our lives with a dog.

Service dog? Most dogs really want to be helpful, if they can just figure out what we're asking for. After all, skills like opening refrigerator doors and dialing 911

🐾 *Every year, Purina, a company that makes pet food, honors heroic animals by adding them to its Hall of Fame. Ally, age four, was walking with her grandmother when she was suddenly attacked by a deer. (The deer was probably protecting a fawn hidden nearby.) Holly, the grandmother's springer spaniel, threw herself between the child and the angry deer, barking and biting. By the time the deer had been scared away, Holly had been badly trampled. This courageous dog suffered a broken leg and lost her sight in one eye, but she saved the child — and won a place in the Hall of Fame.*

don't come naturally to a canine. One owner described teaching his Labrador a new maneuver:

> Just about the time I began shouting like a maniac, out of pure frustration, the dog came back to within a few feet of me and waited till I had calmed down and then, through the expression on her face, told me as plainly as if she could speak, that she didn't really understand what I wanted her to do and that if I could find some way of explaining it, she'd be pleased to do it my way. And that's finally what happened.

Search-and-rescue dog? How many newspaper stories have you read about pet dogs who saved lives? Every year, some of these heroes are honored with medals for their feats: sniffing out the trapped and injured, hauling victims off roads and out of rivers, racing for help and leading rescuers to the scene.

Hunting dog? As any squirrel knows, dogs still have a strong instinct to chase and challenge prey animals. In most breeds, though, the instinct to kill the prey has been inhibited (suppressed) during thousands of generations of living with people.

🐾 Caleigh, an Irish setter, won her place in Purina's Hall of Fame when her owner, Max, had a heart attack. They were out in a field on a cold winter day, and Max collapsed face down in deep snow. Caleigh ran till she found a neighbor shoveling snow, and by barking, leaping, and dashing back and forth, she told him something was terribly wrong. Thanks to Caleigh, paramedics reached Max just in time to save his life.

🐾 This Hall-of-Famer, a black Lab called Stub, was walking with his owner when they met a rescue team searching desperately for two high school students buried under an avalanche. Stub joined the hunt and soon found a pair of gloves, showing the rescue team where to dig for the teenagers. For one victim, rescue came too late. Thanks to Stub's fine nose, though, the other victim was found in time, and her life was saved.

This inhibition was tested in a series of experiments using three types of pups: beagles, coyotes, and beagle-coyote hybrids (halfbreeds). All the pups were raised by people, away from adult canines. Then, one by one, the pups were faced with a live rat.

The coyote pups obeyed their wild nature: they sniffed and prodded the rat, performed a series of play attacks – leaping, barking, growling – and then grabbed the rat and bit it. Most of the coyote pups killed and ate the rat within minutes.

The beagle pups went through the same approach and play attacks, and seemed to be following the same pattern, but not one of them seriously hurt the rat. When these pups reached the point of killing, the inhibition stopped them.

When the hybrid (beagle-coyote) pups met the rats, their reactions were confused and unpredictable. Sometimes they killed the rat, sometimes they didn't – a reminder that when we mix wild canines with domestic dogs, we can't be sure what we'll get. (When the same experiment was done with dingo pups, though, they killed the rats as promptly as the coyotes did – more evidence that dingoes are still wild, despite all their contact with humans.)

Putting on the Dog

Considering how much wolf remains in our dogs, it's strange to see all the pampering some of them get. We may smile at our ancestors who draped their dogs with gold and jewels, but many of us buy dog clothing, whether it's a checked bandanna or a designer jacket with press-on toenails to match. In winter we can coddle our dogs in coats, hats, and boots, or even snowsuits and snowshoes. In summer we can shield them from the sun with caps and sunglasses. They can wear terrycloth robes after a bath, while we brush their teeth with chicken-flavored toothpaste. We can buy them seatbelts for driving, lifejackets for boating, backpacks for hiking, wetsuits for hunting. We can treat them to doggy pastries, gourmet cookies, and water bottled just for dogs. On those special occasions, we can send them doggy gift baskets or have their portraits painted.

We may not have ten thousand servants to care for our dogs, but we still employ people to visit them and walk them. We can send them to doggy hairdressers, to be

🐾 *When Irie, an Irish red-and-white setter, retrieves a toy, he's driven by the same instincts that would send him after a bird or an otter. But the inhibition that stops most dogs from killing other animals doesn't prevent them from chomping up toys — or shoes and slippers!*

shampooed and dyed, perhaps with a pedicure on the side. When we don't have time to be with them, we can send them to doggy daycare. When we do have time, we can spend our holidays with them at dog camp, competing side by side in the matching-swimsuit contest.

At home, we can fit doggy beds with satin sheets and pillowcases. If we tire of tossing tennis balls to be fetched, we can buy a ball-cannon to hurl the balls for us. We can throw birthday parties with turkey-flavored birthday cake. Some people even have doggy weddings, complete with banquet and wedding photos:

> Miss Petite Brabham, the bride, wore a dual-length ivory satin gown trimmed with Alencon lace, and a long veil of French Illusion hanging from a crown of seed pearls.

Miss Brabham and her bridegroom – who wore a white top hat and a black bow tie – were toy poodles.

If little Pixie isn't feeling well, we needn't settle for the veterinarian; we can turn to doggy acupuncture, massage, aromatherapy, herbal medicine, or chiropractic. If the problem seems to be psychological, we can call in a pet psychic or a dog psychologist. If the matter proves serious, it may be time for a dog psychiatrist.

When the sad day comes that we lose our pets, we can have them cremated or buried in a scenic gravesite. If we feel we can't live without them, we can have them

---

Are You Getting a Dog?

All puppies are cute, but owning a dog is a long-term commitment. That's why you should never get a dog until you've thought hard about the responsibility you're taking on.

- Talk to people who have dogs, and ask them to be honest about the hard work of dog-owning.
- Consult dog encyclopedias about the needs and personalities of various breeds.
- Be wary of breeds that are suddenly fashionable; there may not be enough healthy pups to satisfy demand.
- Before you pay someone to breed a dog, visit a dog shelter; many wonderful, lonely dogs are longing to go home with you.
- *Never buy a dog from an unreliable source*; the dog may have been stolen or bred in the misery of a puppy mill.

---

freeze-dried and returned to sit stiffly in our living rooms, obedient at last. And more technology is on the way. Even now, we can have a sample of the dog's blood processed and stored, in the hope that someday a genetically identical clone can be resurrected from the DNA.

Think, for a moment, of our early ancestors learning to share their hard lives with those snarly, sharp-toothed, wolfish pups. Now imagine those ancestors and their new friends set down in a luxury pet store. What on earth would they think of us?

Thinking Like a Dog

One thing that dogs sometimes don't get from us is respect for their dogness. The magic of our enduring partnership lies in the fact that we are two such different species. We diminish that magic when we treat dogs like four-legged people, or babies, or even toys. We come closest to knowing our dogs when we remember their wild instincts, and the strengths and senses they inherit from those wolves who crept up to our cooking fires so many thousands of years ago.

We Talk; They Listen

If we're so smart, why aren't we better at understanding dog talk? We can't even agree on what the basic bark sounds like. To North Americans it's *bow-wow* or *arf-arf*, but the Dutch hear *waf-waf*, the Chinese hear *wung-wung*, and the Czechs hear *haff-haff*.

Psychologist and dog expert Stanley Coren has been listening more carefully, and he's found a wide range of messages, distinguished by subtle differences in pitch (high versus low) and timing. According to Coren, one short, sharp, fairly high bark shows surprise – "Huh?" A bark that's similar but not so high-pitched means "Hello." The same bark a little deeper in pitch means "Stop that!" Add bark-barks, growls, growl-barks, yips, yelps, whines, sighs, moans, bays, and howls, and the dog has a pretty good vocabulary. Too bad we're not paying attention!

When you're talking to a dog – let's call her Brandy – watch her eyes and ears. Try to hear yourself from her point of view. How many of your words does she recognize? Can you simplify your language? Do you choose the same words consistently, to help her learn more? Are you reinforcing your message by using a matching tone of voice and appropriate body language?

Dogs use very pronounced body language. When two dogs meet, watch for the different ways they express their intentions, friendly or otherwise. Notice how they decide which dog is dominant and which is submissive – a reflection of the pack, in which each dog has a certain rank. If Samson is dominant, he'll carry his tail high – and his ears too, if they're not the floppy kind. The submissive dog may roll belly-up, or put open jaws around Samson's neck or face (which seems like a strange sign of submission to us). Samson may even mount the other dog from behind, just to prove his dominance.

If you watch dogs playing in a park, you'll notice other instinctive body language. See that dog who is stretched low, head down, forelegs out in front, tail wagging high in the air? That's a play-bow, and it means "I'm playing now, so when I bark and growl I'm not serious, it's just part of the game."

See that other dog pouncing on a toy with both front feet at once? That's a hunting move called a forelimb stab. The dog still makes this move, even though the final step – the kill – has been inhibited.

🐾 *Responsible dog owners pick up after their dogs. This border collie named Bingo turns the tables; he scoots through the streets of Winnipeg on a skateboard, collects litter that people have dropped, and dumps it in a recycling bin. It's not clear where Bingo learned his neatness, but he got his athletic skills from his mother; she liked to waterski.*

Don't Rush the Nose!

When you take Barkley for a walk, try letting him set the pace. As he puts his nose to work, exploring an invisible world, think of professional tracking and sniffing dogs. Is Barkley ground-scenting or air-scenting? Can you see him cast about for a tempting odor? Can you spot the moment when he finds one? Does he home in on the scent cone, trying to follow it to its source? Maybe he's smelling the steakbones in the garbage that sat here yesterday, or the raccoon that crossed your front step just before dawn, or the motorcycle that roared up this driveway a few minutes ago.

Better yet, perhaps another dog has marked the spot. What goes through Barkley's mind as he inhales the stranger's scent? How much can he learn by smelling another dog's droppings? Here's what one writer imagines:

"Hmm, dog urine, not squirrel or cat. Not mine either, nor a female's. A dominant male, probably an Airedale, healthy, contented as a clam, an adult. What's Rover doing still eating Puppy Chow?"

Don't forget those ears, either. Muffin may be dozing by the window, but watch how she pricks up her ears and focuses when she catches an interesting noise; how she angles her head and works her ears to figure out what it is, and where it's coming from. *Oh, it's just that noisy neighbor again; back to sleep!*

We treasure dogs for the many things they do for us, but they are amazing just for what they are. They have crept out of the wild, into our homes and into our beds. They take part in our lives in a way that no other animal does. We love and trust them, sometimes more than we love and trust people. Yet, somewhere deep in every dog, the wild remains.

What is your dog?

He is your friend, your partner, your defender, your dog. You are his life, his love, his leader. He will be yours, faithful and true, to the last beat of his heart. You owe it to him to be worthy of such devotion.

SOURCE NOTES

Publisher and date are given where a book is Wrst referred to, unless the book is a classic or is included in the Selected Bibliography. Some archaic spellings within quotes have been modernized.

Chapter 1: In from the Cold

The question of how, when, and where dogs developed is still much disputed among experts. This account is drawn from a number of sources, including *Origins of the Domestic Dog: The Fossil Record*, by Dr. Stanley J. Olsen (Tucson: University of Arizona Press, 1985), and *Dog's Best Friend*, by Mark Derr. I am very grateful to Susan Crockford of Pacific IDentifications Inc., who read this chapter at an early stage and corrected my excesses of wishful thinking. The reference to dingoes being almost untrainable is drawn from *The Dog: Its Domestication and Behavior*, by Michael J. Fox (New York: Garland STPM, 1978). The quote from Blondus is cited in *The Lost History of the Canine Race*, by Mary Elizabeth Thurston. The rooster cure for rabies is from *Researches into the History of the British Dog . . .* , by G. R. Jesse (London: Robert Hardwicke, 1866).

Chapter 2: Tools and Toys

The epigraph is from *The Lion Dog of Peking*, by A. C. Dixey (London: 1932), cited in *Reigning Cats and Dogs*, by Katharine MacDonogh. Much of the information about royal pets is drawn from the latter book. The explanation of the bulldog's shape is from *The Animal Estate: The English and Other Creatures in the Victorian Age*, by Harriet Ritvo (Cambridge, MA: Harvard University Press, 1987). The story of the white bear is from *Researches into the History of the British Dog . . .* , by G. R. Jesse. The Meriwether Lewis quotes and other material are drawn from *A History of the Lewis and Clark Journals*, by Paul Russell Cutright (Norman, OK: University of Oklahoma Press, 1976); in some accounts the dog is called Scannon or Seaman. The closing stanza is from "The Pekinese National Anthem," by E. V. Lucas, cited in *The Butterfly Lions: The Story of the Pekingese in History, Legend and Art*, by Rumer Godden (London: Macmillan, 1977).

Chapter 3: Doing What Comes Naturally

All quotes from Robert E. Peary are from his book *Northward over the "Great Ice"* (New York: Frederick A. Stokes, 1898). Matthew Green praised hunting in *The Spleen* (1737); William Cowper criticized it in *The Task* (1785). The section on hunting is based partly on *Dog's Best Friend*, by Mark Derr, and the categories of animal intelligence are drawn from *The Intelligence of Dogs*, by Stanley Coren. The statistics on instinctive behavior are drawn from "Selecting Pet Dogs on the Basis of Cluster Analysis of Breed Behavior Profiles and Gender," by B. L. Hart and L. A. Hart, in *Journal of the American Veterinary Medical Association* 186 (1985), cited in *The Domestic Dog: Its Evolution, Behaviour and Interactions with People*, edited by James Serpell (Cambridge, England: Cambridge University Press, 1995). The quote about New Zealand sheepdogs is from *A Dog's Life*, by Miriam MacGregor, cited in *Dogs: A Historical Journey*, by Lloyd M. Wendt (New York: Howell, 1996). The Richard Bonnycastle quotes are from *A Gentleman Adventurer: The Arctic Diaries of Richard Bonnycastle*, edited by Heather Robertson (Toronto: Lester and Orpen Dennys, 1984).

Chapter 4: Making Sense of Scents

In describing the dog's sense of smell, and its physiological basis, I have drawn from numerous sources, including *The Domestic Dog*, edited by James Serpell; *Dog's Best Friend*, by Mark Derr; *The Encyclopedia of the Dog*, by Bruce Fogle; and "The Intimate Sense of Smell," by Boyd Gibbons, in *National Geographic*, September 1986. The latter is the source of the quote from Bob Noll. The duck egg story and some other smuggling details are drawn from "Hide and Seek," in *Saturday Night*, September 30, 2000. The story of Ralph is based on articles in the South Florida *Sun-Sentinel*, June 24 to June 28, 1997.

Chapter 5: The Nose Knows

The material on pipelines is drawn from "These Dogs Are Doggone Good at Finding Leaks," by K. M. Kostyal, in *National Geographic World*, March 1995. The material on Froy is drawn from *DanishEnvironment*, Internet Edition 5, November 1997 (www.mst.dk/depa/denv). The story of Daisy the beagle is drawn from several accounts in *The National Post* and *The Ottawa Citizen*. The section on bloodhounds is based partly on "We shed 50 million skin cells a day; they make good scents to a hound," by Richard Conniff, in *The Smithsonian*, January 1986, and partly on *The New Complete Bloodhound*, by Catherine F. Brey and Lena F. Reed (New York: Howell

House, 1991). The story of Gracie is based on "Grace under Water," by Donna Jagodzinski, in *Dog Owner's Guide* (www.canismajor.com). The unnamed SAR handler quoted is Sharon Gattas of Riverside Urban Search and Rescue, cited in www.dogsinthenews.com/issues/0109/articles/010918b.htm; the story of Servus is drawn from the same website, 010921a.htm, and from "To the Rescue," by Steve Dale, in *DogWorld*, December 2001. The story of Jeff Eckland is from "Buried Alive," by Susan Reifer, in *Skiing*, March/April 2000. The skier who agreed to be buried was Scott Charter, quoted in *The New York Times Review of Books*, December 14, 1997.

Chapter 6: Dark Days – Dogs Go to War

The epigraph is cited in "The Dogs of War," by Bruce Watsin, in *The Smithsonian*, December 2000. The quote from the British private is cited in *The Dog's Tale*, by Loyd Grossman (London: BBC Books, 1993). The section and quotation about Stubby are drawn from *The Lost History of the Canine Race*, by Mary Elizabeth Thurston. Most material about Guam is drawn from *Always Faithful*, by William W. Putney. Much other material is drawn from *War Dogs: Canines in Combat*, by Michael G. Lemish (Washington: Brassey's, 1996).

Chapter 7: Breaking Down the Barriers

The epigraph is drawn from *The Good Shepherd: A Special Dog's Gift of Healing*, by Jo Coudert (Kansas City, MO: Andrews McMeel, 1998). Most of the material on training guide dogs for the blind is based on work done at Canadian Guide Dogs for the Blind, a non-profit training institute in Manotick, Ontario.

The story about the New York Police Department is from "Dogged Pursuits," by Colin Moynihan, in *The New York Times Magazine*, December 27, 1998. The story about Star is from *Chelsea*, by Paul Ogden. The story of Jarvis is drawn from "Dogged Delivery," by Todd Mercer, in *Dogs in Canada*, March 2002. The story of Pax is drawn from "Out of the Deep Freeze," by Jeannie Marshall, in *The National Post*, November 2, 1999. The story of Ruby is drawn from "Someone Furry to Watch Over Me," by Ian Morfitt, in *The Globe and Mail*, March 28, 2000. Some material, including the stories of Annie and Sam, is drawn from *Dogs That Know When Their Owners Are Coming Home*, by Rupert Sheldrake (New York: Crown, 1999). The story of Dakota is drawn from "A Retriever of All Trades," by Ranny Green in *DogWorld*, March 2000. Bugsy's story is drawn from *Dogs in Canada*, May 2002. The story of Bill and Ben is drawn from "Dog's Best Friend," in *People*, August 24, 1998. The material about Jofi is from *The Pawprints of History*, by Stanley Coren (New York: Free Press, 2002). The rescuer quoted is Bob Sessions of the Federal Emergency Management Agency, cited in DogsintheNews.com, September 2001. The quotes from Arleen Ravanelli and Father Shuley are cited in "Comfort Dogs," by Steve Dale, in *DogWorld*, February 2002.

Chapter 8: Top Dogs

The epigraph is from *The Intelligence of Dogs*, by Stanley Coren. Much of the material about the Lassie dynasty, including the quote beginning "He never hesitated," is drawn from *Lassie: A Dog's Life*, by Ace Collins. The quote about circus dogs, and much of the circus information, is from *Wild Tigers and Tame*

Fleas, by Bill Ballantine (New York: Rinehart, 1958). Scott Taylor's company is Hollywood North, in Langley, British Columbia. Anne Gordon's company is Anne's Animal Actors, in Monroe, Washington. The quote about Fay is from *Fay*, by William Wegman (New York: Hyperion, 1999); for one of Fay's Fairy Tales see William Wegman's *Cinderella* (Hyperion, 1993). Much of the material on the physics of dogsledding is drawn from *The Domestic Dog*, edited by James Serpell. The dogsledder quoted is Lauren Hutton, in *Condé Nast Traveler*, September 2000. David Monson, president of Mush with Pride, was kind enough to review the sled-dog material.

Chapter 9: The Personal Pooch

The epigraph is from "A Snapshot of Rex," in *The Dog Department: James Thurber on Hounds, Scotties, and Talking Poodles*, edited by Michael J. Rosen (New York: HarperCollins, 2001). The quote from the frustrated dog owner is from *The Dog Man*, by Gene Hill, cited in *Mondo Canine*, by Jon Winokur (New York: Penguin, 1991). The experiment with puppies and rats is reported in *The Dog*, by Michael J. Fox. The quote about the dog wedding is from *The Other End of the Leash*, by Berkeley Rice (1968), cited in *The Lost History of the Canine Race*, by Mary Elizabeth Thurston. Stanley Coren's analysis of dog speech, and the translations of "bow-wow," are found in *The Intelligence of Dogs*. The writer imagining his dog's thoughts is Boyd Gibbons, in "The Intimate Sense of Smell." I have not been able to find a source for the closing quote; I suspect that Cyrus, my black mostly-Lab, snuck it in when I wasn't looking.

SELECTED BIBLIOGRAPHY

Booth, Martin. *War Dog* (New York: Simon & Schuster, 1997). A young people's novel about a British war dog.

Collins, Ace. *Lassie: A Dog's Life; The First Fifty Years* (New York: Cader, 1993).

Coren, Stanley. *The Intelligence of Dogs: Canine Consciousness and Capabilities* (New York: Free Press, 1994).

Derr, Mark. *Dog's Best Friend: Annals of the Dog–Human Relationship* (New York: Henry Holt, 1997).

Fogle, Bruce. *The Encyclopedia of the Dog* (London, England: Dorling Kindersley, 1995).

MacDonogh, Katharine. *Reigning Cats and Dogs* (New York: St. Martin's, 1999).

Ogden, Paul. *Chelsea: The Story of a Signal Dog* (Boston: Little, Brown, 1992).

Putney, Capt. William W., DVM, USMC (ret.). *Always Faithful: A Memoir of the Marine Dogs of WWII* (New York: Free Press, 2001).

Ring, Elizabeth. *Performing Dogs: Stars of Stage, Screen, and Television* (Brookfield, CT: Millbrook Press, 1994).

Thurston, Mary Elizabeth. *The Lost History of the Canine Race: Our 15,000-Year Love Affair with Dogs* (Kansas City, MO: Andrews and McMeel, 1996).

Websites

You can read more about some of the dogs, people, and organizations described in this book at the following websites:

Beagle Brigade (United States Department of Agriculture): www.aphis.usda.gov

Central Intelligence Agency (CIA Kids' Home Page): www.cia.gov/cia/ciakids/dogs/index.html

Dog Owner's Guide (online magazine): www.canismajor.com

DogsintheNews.com (news photos): www.dogsinthenews.com

K-9s in Flight (Frisbee Dogs): www.airmutts.com

Lassie: www.lassie.net

Lost-a-Pet Foundation (Kat Albrecht and her pet-tracking dogs): www.lostapet.org.

Rin Tin Tin: www.rintintin.org

United States Customs: www.customs.ustreas.gov/enforcem/k9.htm

ACKNOWLEDGMENTS

I am deeply grateful to the many handlers and other people who were generous with their time and patience, helping me understand the extraordinary partnership they have with their dogs. I'm especially indebted to archeozoologist Susan Crockford, to David Monson of Mush with Pride, and to veterinarian Dr. Greg Usher, who were kind enough to review this material from their various professional points of view, and to do what they could to keep me out of trouble. Thanks also to my dog-devoted publisher, Kathy Lowinger, and to my editor, Janice Weaver.

Most of all – thank you, all you wonderful dogs!

PICTURE SOURCES

Every reasonable effort has been made to trace the ownership of copyright materials. Any information allowing the publisher to correct a reference or credit in future will be welcomed. Pictures not attributed are from the author's collection. For space reasons the following abbreviations have been used:

AKC American Kennel Club
FEMA Federal Emergency Management Agency (U.S.A.)
LOC Library of Congress (U.S.A.)
NAC National Archives of Canada

Page 5: photo by S. D. MacDonald, reproduced courtesy of Canadian Museum of Nature, Ottawa, ON (S95-10614); 6: courtesy of Mary Elizabeth Thurston; 8 (dingo photo): Dave Watts/Nature Focus, Australian Museum (DW-5024); 10: courtesy of Griffith Institute, Ashmolean Institute, Oxford; 19: Kunsthistorisches Museum, Vienna; 21: National Library of Canada (C-38555); 22 *The Westminster Pit*, by Thomas Rowlandson, Toronto Reference Library; 24: Glenbow Archives (NA-1353-26); 26: Provincial Archives of Newfoundland and Labrador (PANL C 3-73); 28: NAC, Canadian National Railways Collection (Accession 1989-455, original item number 39096); 37: LOC (LC-USZ6252064); 40: courtesy of Lorna Coppinger; 41: © Kent and Donna Dannen, courtesy of AKC; 47: illustration by Theresa Sakno, Toronto; 49, 56: NAC; 58, 60: courtesy of Corporal Don Chenel, RCMP; 66: photo by Dan Vice, courtesy of United States Dept. of Agriculture; 69: photo by Fire Marshal Jerry Vigilanti, courtesy of City of Dearborn Fire Department, Michigan; 71: courtesy of United States Dept. of Agriculture (USDA-APHIS 99PPQ0420); 78: © Pets By Paulette, courtesy of AKC; 80: photo by Andrea Booker/FEMA News; 84: courtesy of Anton Horvath, Canadian Avalanche Rescue Dogs Ass'n; 89: painting by Alexander Pope, courtesy of American National Red Cross; 91: LOC (LC-307263); 96: U.S. Navy Submarine Force Museum; 97: courtesy of Tillamook Naval Air Station Museum, Oregon; 99: U.S. Dept. of Defense, Visual Information Center (DNSC9501311); 100: U.S. Dept. of Defense, Visual Information Center (DFST9806299); 111: photos by Michael Milstein, courtesy of Roberta Milstein; 122: photo by Mike Rieger/FEMA News; 124: HB8724, courtesy of Getty Archives; 126: image courtesy of RINGLING BROS. AND BARNUM & BAILEY ® THE GREATEST SHOW ON EARTH ®; 128: LOC (10139-1A 360B); 130: courtesy of Anne Gordon; 131: LOC; 134: courtesy of John Misita, K-9s in Flight; 135: "Waiting to Run," Anchorage Museum of History and Art; 141, 142: courtesy of Nestlé Purina; 144: courtesy of Debby Best; 147: courtesy of *The Toronto Sun*; 148: courtesy of Cheryl Dickie and Anne MacGregor.

INDEX